D0368245

STEALING CHRISTMAS

by

Matthew Sullivan

WET BANDIT

This is a work of fiction. Names, characters, places,
and incidents either are the product of the author's imagination
or are used fictitiously. Any resemblance to actual persons,
living or dead, events, or locales is entirely coincidental.

Copyright © 2016 by Matthew Sullivan
All rights reserved. Published in the United States
by Wet Bandit, Inc., Virginia.

For more on the author, visit matthewsullivanwriter.com
or follow him on Twitter @sullivan_writer,
Instagram @sullivan_writer, or Facebook
facebook.com/matthewsullivanwriter

Cover illustration by Kristie Minke
Cover layout by Crystal Cederstrom
Editing by Lauren Leibowitz

ISBN 978-0-9963020-2-9 (intl. trd. pbk.)
ASIN B01I220FNY (ebook)

The text was set in 14-point Alegreya

10 9 8 7 6 5 4 3 2 1

WET BANDIT
First Edition

For my family and friends.
Thank you for all of your support.

⚜ CHAPTER ONE ⚜

THEY SAY LOVE will make a man do crazy things. And even though I'm still a good five years and change shy of being what almost anyone might consider a man, I know it's true. I know because I've lived it. Over the past month, I've done some of the craziest things I probably ever will do, all in the name of love.

Looking back, there was nothing anyone could have said or done to stop me. The uncontrollable love had burned deep inside me for well over a year, becoming more of an obsession. An obsession not over a girl but a gaming console. The most awesome console ever: the Sony PlayStation 4.

My whole crazy streak started with a harmless game of catch. My best friend Wes Jackson and I were tossing the pigskin in my backyard on what seemed like the perfect Thanksgiving morning in Arlington, Virginia. The sky was as cloudless as it gets, the autumn leaves had just reached their peak, and the weather, while a little on the cool side, was still warm enough that you didn't need anything more than a hoodie. Like I said, it all seemed perfect.

"Hike!" Wes barked, and then dropped back with the football.

I immediately took off, sprinting for the other side of the lawn. "Chuck it!" I screamed in between massive gulps of air, my sprint quickly becoming a lumbering waddle.

Wes just waved me on and shouted, "Deeper!"

I put my head down and fought through the fatigue. As I kept going I could hear Wes giving his own play-by-play.

"The clock is winding down," Wes said hurriedly, as if there were an actual game clock about to expire. "The 'Skins need a touchdown to win. Jackson jukes a defender! He has his man Murphy deep! Does he see him? He does! He lets it fly!"

While I've always thought Wes's play-by-plays were a little over the top, they at least let me know when he was finally gonna throw the ball. He would always "let it fly." And thankfully, he had.

2

The pass was long overdue. My calves were burning, and I was almost in my neighbor's yard. I turned my head to locate the Hail Mary. Everything turned to slowmo as the ball floated through the air, right toward my outstretched hands.

"It couldn't have been thrown any better," Wes shouted in his announcer voice. "It . . . It . . ."

It bounced right off of my hands and landed in my neighbor's shrubs.

I'm sorry. Did I call it a "harmless game of catch"? Yeah, well, that probably wasn't the best way to describe what we were doing, at least not on my end. A harmless game of drops is definitely more accurate.

I dug the ball out of the prickly bushes and whipped it back to Wes. It was one of my classic "rock skippers." That was what Wes liked to call them because the ball would skitter across the grass like a rock skipping on water.

Wes got down on one knee and retrieved the football like a shortstop fielding a tough grounder. He tossed the ball to himself while I jogged back to meet him in the middle of the yard.

"It's pretty pathetic that the 'Skins can't even win when we're pretending," Wes said, shaking his head.

"That's all about to change," I said, a smirk crossing my face as I came to a stop.

"How? Are we gonna start playing as the other team?"

"No! Never," I said, showing my disgust before letting my smile creep back. "But after Christmas, we'll be scoring our touchdowns on Madden, thanks to my new PlayStation 4."

Wes rolled his eyes and groaned. "Please," he begged, "I'm telling you this as your best friend, just let it go."

That's probably not the reaction you were expecting. I bet you'd be way more excited if your best friend told you that they were about to become the proud owner of a PlayStation 4. After all, I'm sure you know just as well as any other kid out there that your best friend getting a new gaming console is basically the same thing as you getting a new gaming console. Or, at the very least, it's like 75 percent the same.

I'm sure Wes figured his skepticism was justified. And maybe it was. I mean, it wasn't exactly the first time that I'd insisted I was getting a PlayStation. Sure, I'd made the same claim before the previous Christmas, and then before my birthday, and then before every holiday thereafter, even the ones that don't traditionally involve presents. But just because no one else (most importantly, my parents) had gotten on board with the idea of getting me a PlayStation for the Fourth of July—it is America's birthday, after all, and you can't have a birthday without presents—didn't mean I was wrong for thinking it made sense, right?

Wes continued, "I know how much you love the PlayStation 4, but haven't you heard the saying, 'If you love something, let it go'? So just let it go."

"Ha!" I said, laughing off his terrible idea. "If that's really true, you should probably let Buster go and see what happens." Buster was Wes's pet Rottweiler, and I knew that he would never even consider just "letting him go." Would he let Buster lick his face right after he'd chewed on a dead squirrel? Sure. I'd seen it happen a couple times. It was nasty.

"That's totally different," Wes said. "I already have Buster."

"So?" I said, sticking to my argument.

Wes took a deep breath and sighed. "I'm just trying to protect you. I don't want you to get your hopes up only to have them crushed again."

"The only thing that's gonna get crushed is anyone who's foolish enough to challenge us on PlayStation Plus."

Wes shook his head. "And you wonder why you've gotten a reputation."

"What are you talking about?" I said. This was news to me.

"Never mind," Wes said, backtracking.

"What's everyone saying?" I asked again, but Wes didn't respond. "Tell me," I demanded. "A kid has a right to know his reputation."

"Fine," Wes relented. "They're all saying you're like the boy who cried wolf. Only instead of wolf, you cry PlayStation."

"Seriously?"

"Yeah."

I couldn't believe it. "Well, first off," I said, defending myself, "I'll be thirteen in five months. So I'm hardly a boy. And second, if you remember the story about that boy, then you also remember that he did eventually see the wolf." I gave a half-smile and tilted my head to drive home my point that I could still see the wolf at some point in the future. Of course, my gesture was totally misinterpreted.

Wes's eyes lit up. "What are you saying? You already saw the PlayStation?"

"Well, no, not exactly," I stammered.

I watched all of the enthusiasm wipe from Wes's face, gone even faster than it had arrived.

"I haven't seen it," I quickly added, "but I did figure out my real problem." I grinned again, aiming to help Wes regain his glimmer.

Wes just scoffed. "What's that, that your parents don't want to buy you a PlayStation?"

"No," I said, not amused by his joke. "My problem is that I've been way too aggressive with my approach. Adults don't like to be told what to do any more than kids do."

"Yeah, I guess that's true," Wes halfheartedly agreed.

"Of course it is. That's why this past month, I've been much more subtle and strategic. An off-the-cuff reference here, a circled newspaper ad there. I even DVRed a couple *Oprah* episodes and paused them on the right commercial. It might not seem like much, but it adds up."

"I applaud your efforts," Wes said. "But that's hardly proof that your parents are getting you a PlayStation, and definitely not reason for any excitement."

"You want proof?" I said. "How's this for proof? A couple days ago, I overheard my dad tell my mom that he was my age when he got his first Nintendo. And guess what? She didn't argue with him either."

"Why would she argue with him? It's not like she'd know how old he was when he got his Nintendo."

"That's not the point," I sighed. "He was obviously using that as an example to show her that I'm old enough because he thinks I should get one. The fact that she didn't argue means that she's at least on the fence. That's a yes and a maybe, which is almost always a yes in parenting decisions."

"Don't you think you might be reaching on that one?"

"Am I? Or am I not reaching at all?"

"I'm pretty sure you are," Wes said. "Regardless, your evidence is circumstantial at best. At worst, it's a lot less than that. Face the facts: Until you actually see the wolf and get visual confirmation, you don't really have anything."

"And how do you expect me to get that? It's not like my parents are gonna just leave the PlayStation box out in the open or forget it in the car."

"I think it's pretty obvious what you gotta do."

"No! No way," I said, knowing full well what he was implying. "I'd rather be pleasantly surprised on Christmas morning."

Wes shook his head in disbelief. "You can't be serious. When has any kid ever been pleasantly surprised on Christmas? Disappointed? Yes. Surprised? No."

He did have a point. While last Christmas had been particularly rough—it didn't help that the wrapped box for the radio-controlled helicopter my parents had actually bought me was the exact size of a PlayStation box—it wasn't like the disappointment was an anomaly. The truth was, I couldn't think of even one Christmas where at least a couple top-of-the-list items hadn't been omitted from my holiday haul. Even so, I was still hesitant to sign up for what Wes was suggesting.

"I don't know," I said. "I don't feel right snooping around the house to try to find where my parents hide our presents."

"You don't have to search the whole house. There's only one place parents really hide presents." Wes paused. He glanced from side to side, making sure no adults were watching or listening, before whispering, "Their bedroom."

"Even worse!" I blurted. I calmed myself and then whispered back, "Did you forget what happened to Gary Templeton?"

Gary Templeton was a former classmate of ours. Starting in first grade, he would sneak into his parents' room every morning and swipe a couple quarters from his dad's change jar. By fourth grade, he was the richest kid in school. Most kids would probably let that kind of wealth go to their heads, but not Gary. He was really cool about it. He would always buy me and some of the other brown-baggers à la carte stuff at lunch.

But everything changed one day, when Gary walked in on his parents doing "parent things." The Gary we knew and loved disappeared that instant. When he finally returned to school after a weeklong absence, he didn't joke around or hang out anymore. He just sat by himself, staring off into space and repeating, "Never again." Weekly trips to the school counselor didn't seem to do much good either. After the year ended, Gary switched schools. No one knows exactly what happened to him after that, but there were rumors that he dropped out before even graduating the sixth grade.

Wes didn't buy my excuse. "Gary Templeton was overconfident, and he got sloppy," he said. "He didn't even check to make sure the coast was clear. He just barged in. That's a rookie mistake. You're older and wiser than he was."

"So I suppose you already know what you're getting?" I said, half-hoping Wes would say that he didn't, and then we could just move on from all our talk about sneaking around. But that wasn't the case.

"You know it," Wes said, beaming. "I'm getting Beats headphones. I got my confirmation last night. Of course, I'm saving my real excitement for Christmas morning. After all, you can't count your Christmas presents until they're unwrapped."

Before I could agree, my mom yelled from the kitchen window, "Mitchell Murphy, it's time to get ready."

My mom is pretty much the only person who actually calls me Mitchell, and that's usually only when she wants me to do something or is punishing me. Everyone else just calls me Mitch, Murphy, or Murph. Although, one time, when I was in fifth grade, a super cute sixth-grader did call me "stud muffin." She might have just said that so I'd give her my chair in the cafeteria, which I gladly did, but I think the compliment still counts.

"I'll be there in a minute," I shouted back to my mom.

"Make it half a minute. You still need to shower." She shut the window as soon as she finished.

For the record, I didn't need a reminder to shower. I can't imagine many seventh-graders do.

But that's just my mom. When I turn forty, she'll probably wish me a happy birthday and then tell me to brush my teeth. She'll definitely tell me to floss.

Wes lobbed the ball to me underhanded. I'm not trying to brag or anything, but I caught it that time.

"I'll call you later," I said.

"Two words," Wes said as he hopped on his bike. He held up a finger for each word. "Visual. Confirmation."

"Yeah. I know. I'll think about it."

"Don't think. Do. For your sanity and mine."

As Wes pedaled away, I couldn't shake his words from my brain. Deep down, I knew he was right. I couldn't wait until Christmas morning. I needed to know if I should stay excited or if I should start bracing myself for the eventual letdown. I needed visual confirmation, and I was determined to get it.

☃ CHAPTER TWO ☃

I SHOWERED AND got ready as fast as I could. I even skipped combing my hair, opting instead for a couple hand-pats to mat my messy brown mop into place, which saved me a few precious seconds. I was still in the process of tucking in the front of my shirt when I peeked out of my bedroom and into the upstairs hallway.

The hallway was completely empty and all of the other doors were shut, just as they'd been when I'd raced upstairs to get ready and also after I'd finished showering. I listened closely for a couple seconds. It was as silent as a school library right after the librarian yells at someone for talking, which was exactly how I wanted it. Silence meant my parents and little brother were still downstairs.

It meant the coast was clear.

Even though I basically had the green light, I held myself back. I knew that only fools rush in, fools like Gary Templeton, and there was no way I was gonna end up like Gary Templeton. I needed to be super-duper-extra-careful. I needed to be completely certain that my little brother wasn't lurking behind one of the closed doors.

It's a well-known fact that younger siblings are responsible for at least 75 percent of the times that their older siblings get in trouble, with a little variance in the percentage based on how spastic the younger sibling is. Since my little brother Connor was on the high end of the spaz scale, even for a six-year-old, I was realistically sitting closer to 90 percent, if not a little higher.

I quietly slipped into the hall, sidled up next to the bathroom door, and gave it a gentle knock. There was no agitated, "I'm in here," or the more common, "Leave me alone!"

After a few more seconds without so much as a peep for a response, I opened the door to make sure that the bathroom was truly empty and that Connor wasn't just playing possum.

There were no possums or little brothers to be seen. I carefully closed the door and then shifted my focus to Connor's bedroom. I followed the same steps that I'd used on the bathroom, knocking and then double-checking, and got the same results.

With my little brother's whereabouts confirmed, or at the very least confirmed to not to be upstairs, it was time to make my move. I tiptoed across the hall to my parents' bedroom door, taking quick glance down the adjacent staircase as I passed by. The stairway and downstairs foyer were both empty, and with that, so was my list of things to look out for. There was nothing left to check. It was now or never, which meant it had to be now because it couldn't be never. I wrapped my fingers around the doorknob, slowly twisted the metallic handle, opened the door, and stepped inside.

I'd barely planted my foot on the carpet in my parents' bedroom when a soft pitter-patter, like something you hear during a light drizzle, stopped me in my tracks. I knew it wasn't rain I was hearing—it was my parents' shower. The noise had been faint enough that the bedroom door had totally muted it. But from inside the room, it was unmistakable. Also unmistakable was what this otherwise soothing sound meant: I wasn't alone.

Even worse, it meant that I was one unfortunate glance from following in the footsteps of Gary

Templeton. No sooner had this realization shot through my brain than I slammed my eyes shut. I let out a slight sigh of relief, thankful that my rapid reaction had, at the very least, saved me from seeing something that couldn't be unseen.

I held the rest of my breath and stared at the back of my eyelids as I waited for the startled voice of one, or both, of my parents, followed some demand to know what I was doing in their room. I hoped that it would be my dad's voice. I figured if it was just me and him, there was a chance I could talk my way out of it. However, I knew if my mom was the one asking the questions, I'd most likely be facing some serious trouble.

My mom has always had the unbelievable ability to secure a confession faster than any of those two-person police interrogation teams you see on primetime TV. I'm sure that even I'd find her talent, the way that she seamlessly jumps between the good-cop and bad-cop roles in the same sentence, impressive if I ever had the chance to see it from the other side of the two-way mirror. Of course, I've only had a chance to see her do her work while I was in the hot seat. There have been plenty of times when I wished that I could ask for a lawyer or maybe plead the Fifth, just like the suspects do on TV.

But I knew better than to bother trying. It's a cold hard truth that Miranda rights and due process don't mean anything to most moms and dads.

I was still working on answers to some of the most likely follow-up questions that my mom might ask when I heard my dad. His voice lifted the giant weight of uncertainty off of my chest. My sense of relief only increased when I realized that he wasn't speaking to me. In fact, he wasn't speaking at all; he was singing, or at least what he considered singing. My mom, on the other hand, always referred to it as an assault on her eardrums, and I tended to agree with her.

I immediately recognized the words and melody, or lack thereof. It was "Sweet Child O' Mine" by Guns N' Roses, my dad's favorite song. As my dad continued to belt his best rendition of the classic song, which also happens to be one of the world's worst renditions, I could hear the water pellets ricochet as he climbed into the shower and then slid the curtain shut.

I simultaneously opened my eyes and exhaled the rest of the breath that I'd been holding in. A smile crossed my face as I confirmed my suspicions: While the bathroom was occupied, the bedroom was actually empty.

As bad as my dad's singing was—and still is—it was music to my ears, and I couldn't have been happier to hear it. Unlike most shower-time Sinatras, who jump between jams, my dad has this thing where if he starts a song, he always has to finish it before he leaves the bathroom.

I'd once heard him tell my mom that it was "disrespectful" to the artist to cut any song short. I'm pretty sure she disagreed, and then my dad said something like, "If Jon Bon Jovi said the same thing, I bet you'd agree," and then chuckled to himself.

Anyway, I knew as long as I started my exit around the same time that he hit his epic mouth-guitar solo, I'd be golden. And since he'd just started, I figured I had at least five minutes to complete my search. That wasn't a ton of time, especially when you take into account the fact that you also have to cover your tracks, and every minute of searching requires at least a minute of covering. However, there was nothing I could do about that except make every second count.

I started my search with the closet. It was the most logical hiding spot. It was pretty big and had a lot of nooks for hiding things. Plus, I'd accidentally seen one of my birthday presents in the closet a couple years earlier, when I went to ask my mom if I could stay at Wes's house.

I wasn't as lucky this time. I didn't find anything. At least not anything that mattered to me. It was just a lot of clothes and shoes.

I quickly made sure the closet was in order and then turned my attention to my parents' dresser. It was the next-best hiding spot. The drawers were just big enough for a PlayStation box.

Unfortunately, all I found were shirts, socks, and my parents' underwear. My initial instincts told me to slam the drawer shut. Thankfully, I was able to fight the urge. The last thing I needed was to create any noise that might get my dad's attention. I gently closed the drawer and then continued my search.

The clock was ticking—four minutes down, one minute to go—and I still had nothing. My heart and mind began to race as feelings of doubt set in. Was I wrong? Was I not getting a PlayStation? Had I fooled myself one more time?

Not wanting to waste my last minute in a panic, I quickly calmed my nerves and asked myself the question that I should have asked before I even started looking: Where would I hide a present if I were my parents?

Bingo! I thought as my eyes landed on the cedar chest at the foot of their bed. It was the perfect hiding spot. Not only do they smell funny, but I'm pretty sure no one even knows what they're for. No kid would ever think to look for their presents in a cedar chest—except me!

The imaginary pats on the back that I'd been giving myself for my genius idea became softer as I dug through the chest and what seemed like endless layers of blankets. The deeper I dug, the only thing I found was more freaking blankets.

My frustration was reaching its peak when I noticed that my dad had already moved on to his mouth-guitar jam session. He kept the riffs coming as he turned off the shower.

That was my cue to bounce. As annoyed as I was that I'd come up empty-handed, I knew had to bail or risk getting caught. I stuffed the blankets back into the chest, shut the lid, and then scurried to the bedroom door. I had my fingers wrapped around the knob and was about to open the door when I heard my mom's voice and froze.

"Connor, why are your pants on your arms?" she asked.

Her words were so clear that I was certain that she was in the upstairs hallway, most likely just on the other side of the door. If not for my six-year-old spaz of a little brother and his inability to properly dress himself, I probably would have already been busted. While the unintentional distraction Connor provided really saved my butt, I knew that it was only a temporary fix. I still needed a way out.

With my mom blocking the bedroom door and my dad preventing any potential bathroom porch exit, there was really only one option I could think of: I was gonna have to jump out the bedroom window.

I booked it to the window . . . and immediately reconsidered my plan. It was terrible for many reasons, the biggest one being that I'd completely forgotten how high of a drop it actually was. Thanks to the slope on the side of the house, it was close to twenty feet. I mean, that's like four times my height!

At that distance, the odds were pretty high that I'd break an ankle from the free fall. Even in the best-case scenario, I'd still end up with a sprain or something. Not to mention the fact that I wouldn't even be able shut the window on my way down. The most realistic way my plan would play out would be with my parents hearing me scream, running to the still-open window, and then finding me rolling in the grass with a jacked-up ankle.

It wouldn't take long, probably seconds, for them to put two and two together.

As I put two and two together, my options went from one to none. There was nothing for me to do but accept my fate.

While I could handle getting caught in my parents' room, I knew there was no way I could let them know what I'd been up to. If there were ever a way to ensure that I wouldn't be getting the PlayStation that I hadn't found, that would be it. And so, I desperately needed an excuse.

My thoughts immediately jumped to Gary Templeton. Not where he'd failed, but where he'd succeeded. After all, he'd stolen change for years before his slip-up. My eyes lit up—that was it! I'd use the Templeton defense and just tell my parents that I was going through my dad's change jar. It was simple enough. And I'd be admitting to doing something wrong, so they wouldn't have any reason not to believe me or to think that I was really up to something else. I figured that all I'd have to do is say that I was sorry and that I'd never do it again, and then take my one-week grounding sentence in stride. It was the perfect plan.

If only life were that perfect or easy. Of course, it isn't and wasn't that day either.

When I rushed to my parents' dresser to grab a few coins to corroborate my story, I discovered that my dad didn't even have a change jar. Unlike me, my great excuse went right out the window. Before I could even come up with a new excuse, I realized my dad's singing had stopped altogether. I jerked my head toward bathroom door, the knob was already turned and the door was just beginning to creak open. Almost simultaneously, came the second creak. My eyes darted to the bedroom door. Through the tiny slit, I could already see my mom's shirt and hair. I just stood there, frozen. No options, no excuses, and no time.

❄ CHAPTER THREE ❄

WHEN I WAS a little kid, and by that I mean about four years ago, I was deathly afraid of looking under my bed. I don't think I actually believed that monsters existed. I just knew that I didn't have 100 percent proof that they didn't, only like 99.99 percent. That super-tiny fraction of doubt was more than enough to keep me from ever taking even the slightest peek under my bed. I think that's also why I initially overlooked it as a hiding spot.

I'd been milliseconds from getting caught when I finally noticed the small space under my parents' king-size box spring and dove for cover. Lucky for me, there wasn't a bunch of stuff stored underneath the bed. I can only imagine what might have happened if I'd crashed headfirst into an old suitcase or something. Well, actually, I know what would have happened. Not only would I have gotten busted, I would have gotten a serious lump on my forehead.

Of course, just because I'd made it under the bed, didn't mean I was in the clear. I knew that until I was safely out of the room, I wasn't actually safe. Which is why I made sure to quiet my breath as much as possible as I tracked my parents' movements by watching their feet.

"We should have left ten minutes ago," my mom groaned.

"Sorry, honey," my dad said. "But you know it takes a lot of work to look this good." He let out a little chuckle.

That was one of my dad's favorite jokes. I knew for a fact he was gonna use it. Just like I also knew exactly how my mom would reply.

"Next time," she said, "I'm fine with you doing less work and looking less good."

Yep, exactly what I'd expected. It's just more proof that old people are nothing if not creatures of habit.

My parents' voices started to fade as my attention shifted to something else. During my frantic dive, my hand had pushed aside the only thing stored under the bed: a small box. It wasn't until my nerves had died down a little that I noticed my hand was still resting on the unknown object.

I carefully moved my fingers across the smooth cardboard, trying to determine the dimensions. By my best guess, it was five inches high and a foot and a half wide, which, in case you weren't aware, are the exact measurements of a PlayStation 4 box.

My thoughts shot in a million directions at once. Could it be? Had I finally found it? I slowly craned my head to catch a glimpse of what my hand had discovered.

It was. I had!

I swear that when I first laid eyes on that beautiful blue and white PlayStation box, there were rays of golden light surrounding it. As I basked in its glory, I even heard a choir of angels sing "Hallelujah!" It might have only happened in my head, but I swear I saw it. Don't believe me? Give me a polygraph. I guarantee I'll pass it.

The next couple minutes were kind of a blur, but I know my parents finished getting ready and then left the room. After they were gone, I took in my PlayStation for another minute. I would have stayed longer, but my mom started to call for me, and I knew my window to escape would close shortly.

I slid out from under the bed and sneaked outside of my parents' room and into the hallway just as my mom stepped into the downstairs foyer.

"Where were you?" she asked. "I've been looking all over."

"I was around. You know, just getting ready," I said with a smile as wide as my face could stretch and then some.

Thankfully, my mom was too preoccupied with getting us out the door to dig further. "Well, you might want to run a comb through your hair again," she said. "Otherwise Grandpa is gonna tell you to go stand in a field."

"Of course," I said, still grinning.

🎁 🎁 🎁

Every kid who has ever lived has had their parents tell them that if they keep making a face, it will stay that way. But that isn't true at all. What actually is true, though, is that if you do make a face for a really long time, the muscles in your face will start to hurt like crazy.

I had a grin glued to my face from the time that I first saw my PlayStation all the way until we were basically at my grandparents' house. It was at least a twenty-minute stretch. It got to the point that my cheek muscles started to twitch from the pain.

I didn't care. I was no longer the boy who cried wolf. I'd seen the wolf, and on Christmas morning the PlayStation 4 would be all mine.

I was imagining how awesome it was gonna be to play my new PlayStation when Connor elbowed me in the ribs. That was our little thing, fighting in the backseat until our dad made us to stop. But that day, I wasn't in the fighting mood. I just ignored him and kept dreaming of my new PlayStation. Connor gave me a few more jabs.

"You're no fun," he whined, finally giving up.

My dad must have thought something was going on because he gave me a curious look from the rearview mirror. "What did you do, Mitch?" he asked. "Did you take Connor's toy?"

"No!" I insisted with a little more enthusiasm than I should have. But I wasn't about to get in trouble, not with my PlayStation on the line. "I didn't do anything," I said, regaining my cool. "I swear."

"Then why are you so smiley?"

"What can I say?" I said with a shrug. "It's Thanksgiving and I've got a lot to be thankful for. I've got my family, my friends, and my health." That was the truth, and at the same time, a complete lie. Sure, I did have all those things, but there was only one thing I was really thankful for, which I wisely kept that to myself.

"You're a funny guy," my dad said.

I just nodded and kept smiling. No one had ever called me funny before, but who was I to disagree with my old man? After all, the guy had been instrumental in making my Christmas dreams come true. He could have said something completely ridiculous, like that salad is way better than pizza, or that the Mets are better than the Nationals, and I would have happily agreed.

"Great, we're the last ones here," my mom said as we pulled into my grandparents' driveway and parked.

If there's one thing my mom doesn't like, and there is actually a lot more than one, it's being the last to arrive to her parents' house on a holiday. My mom is the second oldest of four girls, and the last one to arrive always gets crap from the other three. I'm pretty sure the only time they ever really agree on anything is when they're ganging up on the late one.

As a side note, I have no idea how my grandpa ever survived living in a house with my mom and her sisters. I'm convinced it had something to do with his balding. The family pictures support my hypothesis. He had a full head of hair for the first child, my aunt Jackie, but by the time their fourth daughter, my aunt Denise, joined the party, the top of his scalp was as slick as a soccer ball.

We gathered our things from the car and headed toward the front door. Even from the front porch you could hear the commotion going on inside. There's nothing quite like the holiday pandemonium you get when any large extended family tries to squeeze under one roof.

My parents looked at each other and took deep breaths as they prepared to enter the hornet's nest. "After you," my dad said to my mom with a smirk.

My mom didn't return the smile. She turned to Connor and me and said, "You two can go watch TV or something. Whatever you do, just hang around the kitchen."

"Don't worry about us, Mom," I said. "I'll make sure we both stay out of the kitchen and everyone's hair."

"Thanks," she said.

I pushed Connor inside and we headed for the family room. We didn't make it more than ten feet before we were stalled by our cousin Noah Feinberg.

"Well, hello, Mitch and Connor," Noah said. "Happy Thanksgiving."

"Yeah, Happy Thanksgiving," I said, and then started to make a move around Noah.

But Noah matched my step, blocking our way again. "Did either of you know that wild turkeys tend to be dryer and more gamey than farm-raised turkeys?" he said as he pushed his glasses back up the bridge of his nose.

Noah's parents, and just about everyone else, always called him a prodigy. I was never really sure what that meant, but I always assumed that it was just a polite way of saying that he was really annoying. That's what all of the cousins thought of him. The kid was barely nine and could talk anyone's ear off with all sorts of useless scientific information.

"We do now," I said.

Noah excitedly continued, "You see, it's because farm-raised turkeys are fed more, to fatten them up. While wild turkeys fly more frequently, which leads to a more muscular build."

"Who cares?" Connor said.

It was exactly what I was thinking. But as you get older, you realize you shouldn't say everything you think. That's why sometimes it's good to have a six-year-old around to be the voice of reason.

"I care," I told a noticeably upset Noah, "but we actually have places to be, so let's talk turkey later."

I didn't want to talk about turkeys ever again, I just wanted to get to the family room and fulfill my promise to my mom.

"That would be fantastic," Noah said.

I smiled and gave Connor a shove to get going again. He crashed right into Noah's younger brother, Josh, who came out of nowhere.

"Sorry, little guy," I said.

Josh just kept his eyes locked on the ground. He hardly ever spoke. Aunt Alice and Uncle Robert had adopted Josh from Colombia when he was just a baby. In the seven years since, I'd maybe heard him say five words. For a while, everyone thought he might be mute, but I always figured he just had a hard time getting any words in with Noah around.

"We're gonna go watch cartoons in the family room if you want to come," I said.

Josh finally looked up and nodded enthusiastically. It was a well-known fact that his parents didn't let him watch cartoons, eat candy, or do anything most kids found fun at their house. Whenever I thought my parents were being strict, I used Josh as a reminder that it could be way worse.

"Then let's go, guys," I said. I gave Connor another nudge and we continued toward the kitchen.

I would have taken a different route to the family room, but there wasn't one.

While the delicious aroma of our soon-to-be holiday feast was relaxing, everything else about the kitchen was pure pandemonium. All of my aunts and uncles were packed in there, along with my grandparents, and they were all fighting for space. It was obvious why my mom wanted to keep us from adding to the congestion.

I made sure Connor didn't try to stick around. It's easy for him to get distracted, even when TV is on the table. We made it through the gauntlet of cheek-pinching, said our hellos to Grandpa and Grandma and our aunts and uncles, and then pressed on.

When we finally made it to the family room, I helped Connor and Josh turn on the *SpongeBob SquarePants* Thanksgiving special, then plopped down on the recliner and kicked up my feet. I was confident that the TV would distract Connor until dinner was ready. My work was done. At last I could get back to more important things, like daydreaming about all of the games I'd soon be playing.

I dreamed my way through a game of *Madden*, a couple levels of *Need for Speed*, and most of a *Call of Duty* mission. It's pretty amazing how the imagination works. It was almost like I was playing for real. The big difference is that you can't do any multiplayer gaming in your head. If you can, you might want to see a doctor about that.

My little pretend party was interrupted when some of the other cousins showed up and started to argue over the TV.

"Can we at least check *MythBusters* during the commercial break?" Noah asked.

Connor and Josh shook their heads in unison.

"Come on," Noah pleaded.

"The biggest myth on that show is that anyone cares," said my cousin Claire. "Put on the Kardashians. Their Thanksgiving epi is gonna be amazeballs."

Claire Bower was ten going on thirty, but, like, a really snobby thirty. All she ever talked about was clothes and fashion. Which was really strange because most of the time she looked completely ridiculous. That Thanksgiving was no exception. She was wearing leggings, puffy socks, and a loose sweatshirt that was all cut up.

"I would advise against that," Noah said. "That show kills brain cells."

"Yeah, well, you could use a few less brain cells," Claire shot back.

"Can you all just be quiet?" I said, annoyed. The agitation in my voice caught everyone off-guard and shut them up immediately. "I'm trying to think here, okay? Besides, Connor has the remote, so he gets to decide."

"Yeah," Connor gloated, "I have the—"

Before Connor could finish, another one of our other cousins, Lauren Wetterling, snuck up from behind him and swiped the controller from his hands.

"Hey!" Connor squealed. "What are you doing?"

"I'm putting the Cowboys game on," Lauren said, and then did just that.

Lauren was a real piece of work. Even though she and I were the closest cousins in age, we couldn't have been less close. She hung out with all of the popular kids in our grade, and I mostly just hung out with Wes. In kindergarten, we'd even made an agreement not to tell anyone at school that we were related. Actually, it was less of an agreement and more Lauren ordering me not to tell anyone, or else she would punch me. Only Wes knew the truth because he saw her in the family pictures at my house.

"No way," Connor said as he reached for the remote. "The Cowboys suck."

"Statistically speaking," Noah added, "it is one of their worst years."

"You two suck." Lauren said. She gave Connor a stiff arm to the forehead, knocking him backwards. She turned to Noah to see if he wanted a piece of the action.

Noah just threw his hands up in defeat.

"That's what I thought," Lauren said. "This whole family sucks. Statistically speaking." She cranked the volume of the football game to drown out the others' complaints.

"Come on, Lauren," I said as I got out of my chair. "Just give me the remote."

She didn't give me the remote. Instead, what she gave me was a swift jab to the solar plexus. I doubled over, trying to reclaim my breath.

I've heard people say that someone punches like a girl, but in my experience girls actually punch harder than boys. I think it's because they hit puberty earlier. When it came to strength and height, Lauren had me beat by a lot.

"If any of you want the remote," Lauren said, "you can arm-wrestle me for it."

"Why just arm-wrestle?" Connor snarled. "I'll wrestle you for real. Royal Rumble!"

"I'd own you in two seconds."

"Only one way to find out."

Connor got in Lauren's face, or, really, her stomach, because that's about how high he was on her.

I wanted to play peacemaker, or at the very least save Connor from what was sure to be a serious beating, but it's a lot harder than you'd think when you aren't able to breathe. The rumble was about to go down, and there was no way for me to save my little brother from the pummeling he was about to receive. All I could do was huff, puff, and watch.

⁂ CHAPTER FOUR ⁂

YOU'VE PROBABLY HEARD the tale of David and Goliath. If you haven't, it's about a giant, Goliath, who gets his butt kicked by this little dude, David. It's supposed to be the greatest underdog story ever. A lot of people use it as motivation. But the thing is, everyone focuses on the fact that David was smaller and won, and they totally disregard the fact that he had a freaking sling! That's basically like an old-school gun. I bet if you take the sling out of the equation it's a totally different story, one where the moral is not to mess with giants.

Lauren was a giant compared to Connor, and he didn't have a sling either. The only thing Connor had going for him was—well, nothing, I guess, except for maybe a slightly-higher-than-average pain threshold.

They both took steps toward each other, their fists clenched and teeth gritted.

Thankfully, before it could go any further, our grandma entered the family room. "Turn off the TV. It's time to eat," she said, and then disappeared back into the kitchen.

Connor and Lauren just stared at each other, neither one wanting to be the first to back down.

"Come on, guys," I said, having finally regained my breath. "You both heard Grandma."

After a couple seconds, Connor blinked. Lauren grinned, counting it as a victory. "Looks like you were saved by the dinner bell," she said.

"Or maybe you were," Connor said.

"I'd like to think we all were," Noah said.

"Just so it's clear," Lauren said, "after dinner, we're watching football." She cracked a devious smile, pocketed the remote, and shuffled off for the dining room.

"She's evil," Connor said.

"Yeah," I agreed. I was just glad the crisis had been averted. "Come on," I said as I put my arm around Connor. "Let's get some food."

🎁 🎁 🎁

Every year, our moms try to get everyone to line up and go around the table in an orderly fashion. And every year, it doesn't even come close to working. The whole family attacks the food like a pack of starved wolves. With so many people, getting seconds is never guaranteed. Which means that you need to strike while the iron, or the turkey, is hot, and really load up your plate.

I piled food onto my plate and then got out of the way. As I headed out of the dining room I passed the last of my cousins, Ryan Wetterling, complaining to his mom, Aunt Jackie.

"But I'm a teenager," Ryan said. "I shouldn't have to eat at the kids' table."

"You'll always be a kid to me," Aunt Jackie said. "Maybe next year you can eat with the adults."

Ryan was an eighth-grader and a bit of a meathead. We never really fought like Lauren and I did, but we didn't hang out either. Safe to say, I had no plans of inviting him over to take part in my PlayStation gaming sessions. I was pretty sure he would ask though. Maybe even try to get his mom to talk to my mom. But I'd hold firm. And he'd end up whining, just like he was about sitting with us at the kids' table.

I was the first to grab a seat. I started to dig in to my food but quickly realized that I wasn't really hungry. As I stared at my plate, the food turned into a *Call of Duty* battlefield. My mashed potatoes became a military compound that was protected by a fence of green beans. I used my fork to flip grenade peas toward the gravy center of the potatoes and blow up the enemy base.

"Mission accomplished," I whispered to myself after landing a pea in the gravy.

"Oh my God," Lauren said as she entered the room and caught me playing with my food. "How old are you?"

I wanted to say, "Three months older than you," but I didn't. Instead, I just picked at my food and returned to quietly playing games in my head.

Slowly but surely, the rest of the cousins joined us. Ryan was the last to grab a seat. He dropped his plate on the table. Some of his food spilled off the side of his plate and onto the floor.

"That was smart," Claire said.

"I wasn't trying to be smart," Ryan said as he stabbed his turkey with his fork and then groaned. "I can't believe I have to eat at the stupid kids' table."

"Maybe they can set up a third table," Lauren said. "For kids who think they're adults. They can call it the puberty table."

"Shut up," Ryan said.

"What's puberty?" Connor said.

"Something you won't need to worry about for a long time," I said.

"It's when your body starts to change due to increased hormones," Noah said. "I read a couple books about it. Your voice gets deeper and you have to start wearing deodorant."

"Sounds weird," Connor said.

"No. Weird—" Ryan cut himself off as his voice squeaked. Everyone chuckled, except for Ryan, who cleared his throat and then angrily continued, "Weird is reading a bunch of books and talking about them all the time. Call me when you have facial hair."

"You don't have facial hair," Connor said.

"Oh, yeah? What's this?" Ryan said, pointing to the tiniest of whiskers. It was hardly visible from a foot away, much less from where any of us were sitting.

"Your chin?" Connor said.

"Funny. Look closer," Ryan said.

Lauren and Josh leaned in, examining the contested follicle. "Wow," Lauren said sarcastically. "You have ONE hair."

"I didn't say I had facial HAIRS, did I?" Ryan said. "Besides, you gotta start somewhere. And either way, I'm still too old for this table."

"Yeah, well, I'm too fashionable," Claire said. She eyeballed Connor, Noah, and Josh. "For reals, you three look like your moms dressed you."

"I'm six," Connor said. "Of course she did."

Truth be told, our mom still dressed me sometimes. Although it was really more clothing suggestions than outright dressing. You know, like, what to wear for school pictures and stuff like that. I still tied my own shoes and buttoned my own shirt. Of course, I wasn't about to mention any of that and get involved in the argument. I just kept to myself and my food fortress.

As smart as Noah was, he wasn't smart enough to stay out of the fight. "Yeah," he agreed. "And what's wrong with that?"

"Everything," Claire said. "I was dressing myself when I was three."

"Yeah, well, it shows," Lauren said.

"Says the girl who gets her whole wardrobe at Lady Foot Locker."

"I resent that," Lauren said. "I shop at regular Foot Locker."

"As if that's any better," Claire scoffed.

"It is. Their stuff is better than what you're wearing."

"I'll have you know that this"—Claire gestured

to her clothes—"is how everyone in L.A. dresses."

"Last time I checked," Ryan said, "this isn't L.A."

"How exactly did you check?" Claire said. "I bet you can't even find L.A. on a map."

"I can," Noah said.

"No one cares what you can do," Ryan said.

Noah slouched back in his seat.

This was all getting out of control. And while I'd told myself to stay out of it, I decided that I had to throw a little water on this foolish fire. "Guys! Girls!" I said. "It's Thanksgiving. Can't we all just get along?"

They all looked at me like I was insane. You would have thought I told them I was marrying Jennifer Lawrence or had just been drafted in the NBA. Apparently, I'd given them something that they could all agree on. "NO!" they shouted at the same time.

My water ended up being more like gasoline.

"Jeez, you're such a loser, Mitch," Lauren said and rolled her eyes.

"Hey!" Connor shot back. "Don't call my brother a loser, you big bully!"

I turned to Connor and was about to thank him when I noticed that he wasn't quite finished. The little David had found his sling and was preparing to slay the giant. He held his spoon cocked back with his thumb, a single green bean in the center, ready to fire. He looked at me, as if waiting for the order. My first inclination was to stop him. As the older brother, I was always trying to keep him out of harm's way, no matter how often he got on my nerves. But Lauren had been especially mean that day, so instead of having him to stand down, I just shrugged.

What happened next was like the first shot at Fort Sumter, or the assassination of that Archduke of Earl or whatever his name was. Connor launched the green bean at Lauren. The tiny projectile exploded as it hit her square on the forehead.

"Are you kidding me?" Lauren growled. Her face turned redder than the cranberry sauce on her plate as she fumed. She loaded up a spoonful of mashed potatoes and catapulted them back at Connor.

Connor ducked at the last second. The potatoes splattered on Claire's sweatshirt. "OMG!" she screamed. "This is haute couture!"

To this day, I still have no idea what that means, and I refuse to Google it. All I know is that Claire flung a massive turkey leg in retaliation.

The leg ricocheted off of Ryan's chest, and then he flashed one of the most wicked grins I've ever seen in person. I knew that whatever he was planning, it wasn't good. I quickly grabbed my plate and backed as far away from the table as possible.

"Game over, runts," Ryan said. He unloaded a barrage of food, hurling whatever he could every which way.

All of the other cousins returned fire.

I just shook my head as I watched it unfold. It was obvious they were all gonna get in big trouble. They didn't see it, but I did, and I had no intention of going down with any of them.

🎁 🎁 🎁

Needless to say, it didn't take long for all our parents to hear the commotion and come sprinting into the room. Connor got in one last shot of stuffing before my mom yanked his arm.

Our parents lined us up shoulder-to-shoulder, like we were in some police lineup. Everyone was covered in mashed potatoes, gravy, and every other side dish that stuck, except for me. My clothes were as clean as they'd been when I climbed into them.

My grandma picked up what remained of her turkey-shaped gravy bowl, which had fallen off the table in the middle of the melee and shattered. "This was a wedding gift from my mother," she said as she started to tear up. My grandpa comforted her.

I felt terrible. Even though I didn't personally break the gravy bowl or even partake in the food fight, it hurt to see her so sad and to have her think that I was even partially responsible. The rest of the cousins seemed to feel pretty bad about it too. They all looked down at their feet.

Ryan and Lauren's mom, Aunt Jackie, shook her head at them. "I don't believe this," she said. "You two are the oldest."

Somehow, she always forgot that I was actually older than Lauren, but at that moment, I wasn't too concerned about correcting her. She had a long-standing reputation for being "the strict aunt." She probably got that way from being the oldest of the sisters. My mom said she was always bossy, even as a kid. I learned from a very young age to be on my best behavior around Aunt Jackie.

Aunt Jackie turned her attention to just Ryan. "And you wanted to sit at the adults' table. Do you think there are food fights at the adults' table?"

"Probably not," Ryan mumbled, still looking at his feet.

"Of course there aren't. Both of you should know better." She put her hands on her hips and shot them both an icy stare.

It was obvious where Lauren had inherited her ability to strike fear with one look. It was too much for me. I had to turn away.

"You know what?" Aunt Jackie said as if she'd just had the perfect idea. "To help you two learn a lesson, I'm taking away all of your Christmas presents."

With that, there was a loud gasp. It was like every molecule of oxygen had been sucked out of the room. All of the cousins' heads shot up and eyes went wide.

I've heard people say, "I wouldn't wish that on my worst enemy." I always said that it depended on what the "that" was. At the time, Lauren was the closest thing I had to a worst enemy, and I'd wished a lot of things on her. Mostly stuff like getting grounded, losing at sports, for once, or catching a cold—not like a serious cold, just a mild one. But even with our bad blood, I never would have wished that she'd lose her Christmas presents. That would be going too far.

However, it clearly wasn't too far for Aunt Jackie. Ryan and Lauren reacted exactly how you would expect any kids to react: They threw massive fits.

"You can't take away our presents!" Ryan screamed.

"Yeah!" Lauren angrily agreed.

"I'm your mother, I can do whatever I want," Aunt Jackie said firmly. "I'll give your gifts to kids who actually deserve them. Kids that know how to behave."

If we were all caught off-guard by Aunt Jackie, which, given her reputation, we probably shouldn't have been, we were completely blindsided when Claire's mom, Aunt Denise, spoke up.

"Me too," Aunt Denise said. "And not because I need to follow other people's parenting, but because I want to."

The youngest of her siblings, Aunt Denise is constantly defending herself and her decisions to the other sisters, especially Jackie.

"WTF, Mom?!" Claire shouted.

"Don't you swear at me, little lady," Aunt Denise said. "I can take away your birthday presents too."

That quieted Claire real quick, which gave Noah and Josh's mom, Aunt Alice, a chance to weigh in. "I think this is a great idea," she said to her sisters. She turned to Noah and Josh and added, "Not only will it teach the both of you a lesson on how to behave, it will teach you not to place too much value on your possessions."

If you couldn't guess from that, or her anti–cartoon-and-candy stance, Aunt Alice was kind of a hippie weirdo. Oddly enough, for someone who didn't value possessions, all her husband, Uncle Robert, ever talked about was his hybrid car and its "MPGs."

"This is more a question of semantics," Noah said in a surprisingly calm tone, "but only Christmas presents were mentioned. How might this affect our Hanukkah presents?"

I'd always been jealous of Noah and Josh for having the two holidays. It didn't matter that their parents always got them crappy gifts. I figured it was at least partly because Noah only asked for crappy gifts, like microscopes, chemistry kits, and things like that. But the things I would have done with twice the presents . . .

Aunt Alice looked to Uncle Robert, who just shrugged. "Same deal," Aunt Alice said.

"As I assumed," Noah said. "I just wanted to confirm."

I definitely wasn't jealous of Noah and Josh anymore.

While I wouldn't have wished that fate on my cousins, I couldn't say that I really felt that bad for any of them either. After all, I'd tried to get them to stop fighting, and they just yelled at me. In a way, they got what they deserved. They'd made their beds and peed in them, and now they had to lie in those beds.

Yep, that's pretty much how I felt . . . right up until the moment I saw all of my aunts turn their attention toward my mom.

☆ CHAPTER FIVE ☆

MY MOM TOOK in her sisters' stares for a moment and then turned to Connor and me. She didn't look nearly as upset as my aunts had when they handed down their punishments, or even when she would usually punish me. If anything, she looked conflicted. It was a good sign. It meant I had a chance.

I knew my best defense would be a good offense, to cut her off and present my argument before she could say anything. That's exactly what I did. "Hold on a second!" I insisted. "I had absolutely nothing to do with this. Just check out my clothes. They're totally clean. See?" I spun in a circle to show off how—unlike all of the other cousins—I was completely food free.

My mom paused for a second. I could tell the wheels in her head were turning and hoped they were turning in my direction. Each passing moment gave me more confidence that she couldn't take away my presents now that she knew the facts. I mean, she couldn't deny the facts, right?

Just when I was certain that my mom was about to let us off the hook, Aunt Jackie cleared her throat with the force of an old garbage disposal. I threw out my best puppy-dog eyes to counter Aunt Jackie and keep my mom's gaze on us.

It didn't work. My mom turned back to her sisters, who hadn't stopped glaring at her.

What happened next is proof that peer pressure isn't just something kids have to deal with. In fact, it's probably the biggest unspoken problem facing parents these days—that, and not knowing how to pack a good lunch.

When my mother turned back to Connor and me, there was a totally different look in her eyes. It was unlike anything I'd ever seen. I don't want to say she was possessed because I'm pretty sure she wasn't, but I didn't even recognize her.

"You might not have been a part of the fight," my mom said, "but you didn't do enough to stop it either."

Hearing her say that blew me away. I didn't realize it was my job to be the kids' table police. I thought being neutral was always an acceptable position. If we'd lived in Switzerland, I'm sure it would have been enough. Unfortunately, we didn't, and apparently, neutrality wasn't good enough for my mom.

"But Mom," I said. "I'm getting—"

I was dangerously close to mentioning the PlayStation 4 and outing myself. Thankfully, I stopped short of spilling the beans. If my mom knew that I knew what my present was, it would have sealed my fate for sure.

"What are you getting?" my mom said.

I froze, swallowed hard, and said, "Good grades."

"Yes, you are. And we expect you to get good grades. Just like we expect you to behave yourself."

"But—"

"No buts. I'm giving yours and Connor's presents to charity too."

My body went stiff as the words passed through my ears and bounced around in my head. I was in complete shock. Just three hours earlier, I'd gotten my visual confirmation. I'd seen my PlayStation. And now, it was being stolen from my stocking. It was the ultimate in high to low. How I didn't set the world record for the youngest kid ever to have a heart attack is still a mystery to me.

🎁　🎁　🎁

After I was forced to help my cousins clean up the mess they'd made, we hopped into our car and headed home. That was the end of our so-called holiday.

I didn't say a single word during the car ride or after we got back home. By then, my shock had subsided and turned to anger, anger at my entire family and the complete mockery of the parental judicial system. I mean, punishing me for "not doing enough" was one thing, but punishing me worse than all of the others who were actually involved in the food fight was another.

And there was no doubt in my mind that my punishment had been more severe. My cousins couldn't have been getting gifts as awesome as mine. Losing my PlayStation was like getting a life sentence while they were just getting little slaps on the wrist. The punishment didn't fit the crime any more than I fit into my old childhood onesie.

Without even being told to, I went straight to my room.

"Good night," my parents said softly from my doorway as I climbed into bed.

I just rolled away and waited for them to leave.

I didn't speak for the rest of the Thanksgiving weekend. I just stayed in my room on a hunger strike. It wasn't a real hunger strike, like the ones Mahatma Gandhi used to do. I'd sneak a snack any chance I got, but only when my parents weren't looking. Still, as far as they knew, I'd gone Gandhi.

Going Gandhi was my go-to way to get at back my parents after they punished me. I was determined to stick it out as long as possible. I wanted my parents to think that I could keep it going for the next six years, until I went off to college. Of course, there was no way I would, but I was able to make it through the rest of the weekend without getting caught eating or speaking.

The Monday morning after the break, I told Wes about everything that had happened as we trudged down the hall to our lockers.

Wes shook his head. "Man, now I totally understand why you didn't return my calls. To be honest, I don't even know how you made it to school. I'd probably still be in bed."

"Yeah, well, my parents made me," I said.

"Of course they did, but what's their leverage? I mean, they already took everything from you."

"They really did. And I was so close. The PlayStation was right at my fingertips. I literally touched it with my fingertips."

"I know plenty of kids who have been threatened with a presentless Christmas. But not one kid in the whole history of kids has ever had all of his presents taken away. It's cold-blooded. No. It's criminal. No. It's all of the above and then some."

"Yeah, well, as much as I blame my parents, it's really all my cousins' faults."

"I don't know about the rest of your cousins"— Wes stopped and stared off in a daze—"but I'd have a hard time staying mad at Lauren, even if she did cost me a PlayStation. She's just too dang hot."

I traced his gaze. Across the hall were Lauren and her pack of friends from the girls' basketball team. I gave Wes a light elbow to the ribs, jolting him from his daydream. "Come on," I said. "She's my cousin. Besides, you'd think differently if you knew her like I do."

"I don't know. I kinda like them feisty."

"I don't even know what that means."

"Neither do I," Wes said. "Neither do I."

Lauren caught us looking in her direction. She glared back at us. I turned my head as fast as I could, nearly giving myself whiplash.

Wes just grinned and gave her a wink and a nod.

"Come on," I said. I nudged Wes, and we continued to our lockers.

🎁 🎁 🎁

Later that night, my parents demanded that we have a "family dinner." Everyone ate quietly, except for me. I didn't touch my plate. My parents had caught me breaking my vow of silence shortly after I got home from school, but that only strengthened my desire to keep the facade of the hunger strike going.

After a while, my mom tried to put an end to the awkwardness. "So . . ." she said, testing the waters before getting going. "Mrs. Johnston called and said they'd love to have you play Joseph in the Christmas pageant again." She smiled like she'd delivered some kind of great news.

"Awesome!" I said, pretending to be excited. "I have an idea for the pageant too."

My mom's face lit up even more. "Really?"

"Yeah. I was thinking Mary and Joseph could wake up on Christmas morning and find that Jesus isn't there, just like our presents."

The excitement immediately disappeared from my mom's face. "Okay," she said. "I take it you don't want to be in the pageant."

"Duh," I said as I rolled my eyes.

"Don't talk to your mother like that," my dad said.

The room went silent. It stayed that way for the rest of dinner. I flicked my green beans around my plate for another ten minutes before my parents finally let me leave the table.

Connor and I went downstairs to watch TV. I didn't actually want to watch TV, I just didn't want to be around my parents.

I plopped down on the couch and vented aloud. "What the hell was she thinking, asking me to be in the Christmas pageant? That's like rubbing salt in my wounds."

I looked to Connor, who had already turned on an episode of *Ninjago* and, like always, was doing his best to match the karate moves on the screen. I couldn't believe it. He wasn't even fazed. It totally blew my mind. "Hey," I said, getting his attention. "How are you not angry about losing your Christmas presents?"

"Easy," Connor said as he executed a karate chop, followed by a couple other wild moves. "We only lost our presents from Mom and Dad. We're still getting the ones from Santa."

Of course that was why he was so upbeat.

Being the responsible older brother, there was no way I was gonna ruin the miracle of Christmas for the little guy. I'll never forget when I found out the truth about Santa or when I found out that wrestling was fake. Learning those two things not only changed the way I looked at Christmas and wrestling, it changed the way I looked at the whole world.

"Oh, yeah," I said. "I forgot about that."

"I didn't. Plus, I realized last year that Mom and Dad don't even get us what we ask for, anyway. That's why this year, when Mom wrote my letter to Santa, I made sure to have her ask him for all the stuff I really wanted. I only asked Mom and Dad for the things they get us every year. All the presents they took away, are just the presents that I don't even want."

"Wow. That's actually pretty smart of you."

"We don't do much work in first grade. I had a lot of time to think about it," Connor said. His eyes lit up as he got an idea. "You should totally ask Santa for your good stuff. Did you already send him your list?"

"Not yet," I said. "I'm still figuring it all out."

"Well, you better hurry up. You know it takes a while for mail to get to the North Pole."

"Good point."

Just as soon as I finished speaking, the TV show switched to a commercial for the PlayStation 4. We both turned our attention to the screen. In the commercial, two best friends played various games and had an awesome time. I used to love that commercial. But at that moment, it was just a harsh reminder of all the joy that I wouldn't be having.

Connor jumped up and down on the couch. "You need to ask Santa for a PlayStation 4!" he shouted. "He'll get it for you. You can let me play it with you. It'll be so awesome!"

"I can't watch this," I said. I got up from the couch and headed toward the stairs.

"Hey! Wait for me!" Connor screamed as he jumped off of the couch and chased after me. "I can't be in the basement by myself."

I climbed the stairs with Connor nipping at my heels. As we got near the top, I overheard my parents talking while they finished doing the dishes. I stopped a couple steps before the closed door and turned to Connor. "Shhh," I whispered with my index finger to my lip.

Connor zipped his lip, buttoned it, and threw away the key.

We eavesdropped on the rest of our parents' conversation.

"So you talked to your mom?" my dad said.

"Yes," my mom said. "She said we could bring the presents over whenever we want."

"And everyone else is bringing their presents to your parents' house too?"

"Yeah. That's the plan. We all talked and decided it was the best way to handle this."

"I think so too," my dad said.

Up until that point, I'd held out the smallest sliver of hope that my hunger strike would convince my dad to convince my mom that I should still get my PlayStation. Hearing my dad agree with their plan, that little hope died. I was so furious that I had to bite my tongue to keep from screaming.

My dad continued, "Just let me know when you want me to take them over."

"The earlier, the better," my mom said. "But as long as they're there by Christmas Eve, we're fine."

Connor and I waited for a more than a minute after our parents had finished up and headed upstairs before we entered the kitchen from the stairway.

"I can't believe they're taking all the toys to Grandma and Grandpa's," I fumed as I paced the length of the kitchen. "And why would they need them there by Christmas Eve? Why hold off on the donation? Just get it over with."

"I don't know," Connor said with a shrug.

That's when I spotted the Toys for Tots flyer pinned to the refrigerator door. I ripped the flyer from the fridge and held it for Connor to see. "This has gotta be why!"

Connor stared blankly at the flyer. "You know I can't read yet. What does is say?"

"It says the Toys for Tots are now doing Christmas Eve pickups."

"That's nice of them."

"No," I corrected him. "Nice is what I've been my whole life. And look where that's gotten me. Nowhere!" Just then, something very naughty popped into my head: a way to get our toys back. I couldn't help but grin.

"What are you smiling about?" Connor asked.

"I think I figured it all out," I said. "And if those tots think they're getting any of our toys, they better think again. Call all the cousins."

"Seriously?" Connor said. "I don't know any of their phone numbers."

"Fine. I'll call them," I said, my grin growing as the plan percolated in my mind.

☆ CHAPTER SIX ☆

BEFORE I WAS known for being the kid who cried PlayStation, albeit without my knowledge, most kids in school knew me as the kid with the coolest tree house. That's not a bad reputation to have in the third grade, but I've found it doesn't carry nearly as much weight once you hit fifth grade, and it only goes down from there.

I called all of my cousins and told them to meet at my tree house the next day. They were all reluctant at first, but when I informed them that it was about our Christmas presents, they quickly changed their tunes.

"Looks like everyone is here," I said as Josh and Noah, the last ones to arrive, climbed inside the tree house.

"Are you finally gonna tell us why we're here?" Lauren groaned.

"Isn't it obvi?" Claire said as her teeth chattered. "He wants us to freeze to death."

The weather had recently taken a turn. You could already see your breath and everything. But the tree house was the best place for us to meet. What it lacked in central heating, it made up for in privacy.

"That's the last thing I want," I said. "I called you all here because last night I overheard my parents talking about our Christmas presents. It turns out that all of our parents are dropping them off at Grandma and Grandpa's." I retrieved the Toys for Tots flyer from my coat pocket and handed it to Claire. "Pass that around. At 9 p.m. on Christmas Eve, Toys for Tots is picking up our presents. And on Christmas morning, some other kids will be playing with our toys. That is, of course, unless we do something about it."

The cousins looked at me like I was speaking Greek, except for Noah, who had taught himself a little Greek and probably would have understood if I had actually spoken Greek. But he looked at me with about the same amount of confusion.

"What are you suggesting we do?" Claire asked.

"On Thanksgiving, our parents decided to rob us of Christmas," I said. "What I'm suggesting is . . . we steal it back."

When I'd practiced my little speech in front of my bedroom mirror, I anticipated it ending with a really big finale. Like all the cousins would start cheering and then maybe pick me up on their shoulders. Yeah, that didn't happen. They just looked at me for a moment in stunned silence.

"Well . . ." I said, hoping to get the responses rolling.

"He's joking," Noah said to the others with a nervous laugh. "He has to be joking." He looked me in the eyes, no longer laughing. "You're joking, right?"

"I'm not joking," I said.

"What's the plan?" Ryan said.

"I don't actually have a full plan yet," I said.

"Of course he doesn't," Lauren chirped.

"I wanted to make sure everyone was on board before I came up with one," I said. "But with the Christmas Eve deadline"—I retrieved a red Sharpie and the tree-shaped Advent calendar, which I'd purchased from the Dollar Store, from my backpack and circled Christmas Eve—"that gives us just over three weeks to plan, prepare, and execute the heist. That should be more than enough time."

My sixth grade Language Arts teacher always said people like visual aids for speeches. I don't know if it was that or the chocolates behind each of the twenty-three yet-to-be-opened tabs or something totally different, but the calendar seemed to get their attention.

"So what do you guys think?" I said.

The cousins looked to each other, silently gauging the group's interest. Finally, Ryan stepped up. "I think your plan is pretty weak," he said.

"Of course it is," I said. "I just told you I was waiting to figure out the specifics of the plan."

Ryan held up his index finger to quiet me.

I shut my mouth and did my best not to roll my eyes.

"I also question your maturity," Ryan added.

I'd always questioned a lot of things about him, but I needed him on the team. So instead of firing back an insult of my own, I just nodded in agreement.

"I'll do what I can to work on that," I said.

"That's good enough for me. I'm in."

"Great. Anyone else?" I said. "Simple yeses are acceptable too. In case anyone was wondering."

"My parents are crazier than Kanye's fashion designs if they think I'm just gonna let them take my presents," Claire said. "I'm in too."

"Awesome," I said, clapping my hands to pump up the rest of the group. "Two down. You're next, Noah. Want to make it three?"

"I don't know," Noah said.

"What's not to know? You and Josh had two holidays' worth of gifts taken from you. You've lost the most. Which also means you got the most to gain."

Noah looked down at his feet, still on the fence.

"Come on," I said, "we could really use your smarts on the team."

Noah lifted his head, a sparkle in his eyes. "We're gonna be, like, a team?"

"Not 'like' a team," I said. "We are a team."

"I've never been part of a real team before."

"Well, now's your chance."

Noah's face lit up like, well, a Christmas tree. It turned out that just because he was almost always by himself, it didn't mean that he wanted to be.

"Okay! I'm in!" Noah said.

"Now we're cooking," I said. "Josh? I saw you checking out the Advent calendar. I know your parents don't let you have candy. I'll let you have every piece of chocolate in the calendar if you help out. What do you say?"

Josh just looked at me.

I quickly realized how foolish it was to ask a kid who never talks what he says. "Forget that," I said. "You don't have to say anything. Just smile if you're in."

Josh grinned from ear to ear. He was on board. That left just one person.

"Lauren?" I said.

She shot me one of her evil-eyed looks. I couldn't help but cringe a little. I was like Pavlov's dog. Only instead of getting food, that glare was usually followed by a stinging punch. Thankfully, no blows were thrown.

Lauren's face softened. She shook her head and sighed. "Something must be wrong with me if I'm actually agreeing with you," she said. "But this is probably our only option."

"Perfect!" I said, relieved that she was in and also that I avoided a walloping. "That's all of us."

"Not quite," Ryan said. "You forgot about him." He gestured to Connor.

"Don't worry about Connor," I said. "He's in."

"No, I'm not," Connor quickly countered, completely throwing me for a loop.

"Uh, what do you mean you're not in?" I asked.

"I already told you," he said, "I'm getting my good stuff from Santa."

"Awww," Claire said, "that's so cute you still—"

"Shhh!" I said as I shot her a look to keep quiet.

"You guys should all go straight to Santa," Connor said. "It's a lot easier than this crazy heist thing." Without another word, he climbed out of the tree house.

All of the cousins turned to me with concerend faces.

"What are you gonna do about him?" Lauren said.

"Nothing," I said. "We're fine. There's still more than enough of us to pull this off."

"Yeah, there are, but he knows too much. He's a liability."

"That is factual," Noah agreed.

"Plus, he's like two years old," Ryan said.

"He turned six a couple months ago," I corrected him.

"Same difference. Either way, he needs to be taken care of."

"Whoa. What do you mean, 'taken care of?'" There was no way I was gonna physically pressure my brother into keeping quiet.

"He just means we need to get him on the team," Noah said. "Right? That's what you mean."

"Yeah," Ryan agreed."

"SMH," Claire said. "Why don't you just tell him—"

"Shhh!" I said out of habit.

"Don't shush me!" Claire fired back. "He's not even here."

"Sorry. But that's just not an option. I'm not gonna ruin Christmas for him any more than it already has been."

"Well," Lauren said, "you gotta convince him to join us one way or another."

I thought about it for a second. They were definitely right. The last thing we needed was to start off the mission with a loose end.

While there was no way I was gonna ruin the magic of Christmas for my brother, I realized I could use it to my advantage.

"I have an idea," I said. "I just hope, for my sake, there's no such thing as karma."

🎁　🎁　🎁

Full disclosure, I'm not exactly sure what karma is. But I have heard a lot of people use that line when they're about to do something they probably shouldn't.

I've also heard people say that karma is a B-word, but they might have just been talking about a person named Karma who's a jerk. If that's the case, I know a bunch of people who should've been named Karma.

71

When I found Connor in the living room, he was just getting settled in to his cartoons. "Did everyone else leave already?" he asked.

"No, not yet," I said. "I just really needed to talk to you. See . . . I wasn't 100 percent honest with you before."

"About what?"

I bit my lip and looked away, using the same acting chops I'd mastered in the Christmas pageant the year before to let Connor know how serious the situation was. "It's better if I show you," I said.

"Okay," Connor said, unsure of what to make of it all but clearly nervous.

I led Connor into the study, sat down at the computer desk, and opened our mom's email account.

"I didn't want to show you this before," I said, "because it's against the law to read other people's emails, but you need to know the truth. Go ahead, read that." I tapped the screen.

"You know I can't read all those words," Connor whined.

Of course I did. That was the most important part of selling my plan. My terrible, horrible plan. "Oh, yeah," I said. "Sorry. I forgot."

"Can you read it for me?"

"Of course. It's an email from Mom to Santa."

Fear washed over Connor's face. He swallowed hard. "Well, what does it say?"

"It says, Dear Santa . . ." I didn't have the next part planned out, so I had to make it up on the fly. "I'm sad to report that my two boys have been extremely naughty this year. So naughty, that we decided to donate all of their presents to charity. While I realize that you have your own policy, with the coal and all, I'd encourage you to do the same and donate their presents. Hopefully, this will teach my children a lesson. We look forward to your visit next year and hope everything is going great up north. Merry Christmas, Karen Murphy."

"Did Santa reply?" Connor asked, a tiny shred of hope left.

"Yeah," I said and looked away, not wanting to see my little brother's face as I drove the nail through his Christmas coffin. "Santa just said that it worked for him and that he'd give our presents to charity too."

I quickly minimized the email just in case Connor was actually able to make out any of the words. I wasn't feeling too good about myself. That feeling only grew stronger when I turned back to Connor.

He had the same zombie-like stare you usually only see on the faces of professional athletes when their teams lose the championship on a last-second play, which was also their fault.

"This isn't fair," Connor said, his head shaking side to side in total disbelief. "I don't have Santa's email address. I don't even have my own email address!"

"Me either," I said, suppressing my feelings of guilt as best as I could. "So, do you want in now?"

❄ CHAPTER SEVEN ❄

IN MY SHORT time on this Earth, I've done a handful of things I'm not proud of. Who am I kidding? We're all kids here, or at the very least have all been kids at one time or another, and we've all done a lot of stuff we're not proud of. Even so, the lie I told Connor that night is near the top of my list, if not at the top. I'm pretty sure that when it comes time to make my case to Saint Peter, it's probably gonna be the first thing he asks me about. Hopefully, I'll have a good answer by then.

As I climbed back into the tree house, it was obvious from the expressions on my cousins' faces that they were hoping for a good answer too. They'd been waiting with bated breath and were eager to find out if I'd been able to sway my little brother.

After a second, Connor poked his tiny head through the hatch door. "She emailed Santa," he said as he pulled himself inside the tree house. "My mom emailed Santa! Can you believe that?"

"No way," Ryan said as he and all of the cousins shook their heads in feigned disbelief. "That is not cool."

"Yeah," Claire agreed. "That's totes cray-cray."

"Tell me about it," Connor said.

I could see this griping going on for a while, so I nipped it in the bud. "Let's not forget that all of our parents did something horrible." I pinned the Toys for Tots flyer to one of the tree house walls and gave it a slap with my palm. "And righting that wrong is what we need to focus on. Now that we're all on board, I'm gonna need a day or two to figure out what—"

"Whoa! Hold on a second," Lauren interrupted. "I agreed to be part of this, but I never signed off on you calling all the shots."

"Are you serious?" I said, surprised. Although, I really shouldn't have been. "This whole thing was my idea."

"That's great. Good job, you deserve a cookie," Lauren said with the smuggest look possible. "But just because you had the idea doesn't mean you're the best one to run the show. When have you ever led anything?"

I thought about it for a second, trying to come up with any time where I'd really showcased my leadership so that I could stick it to her. Unfortunately, the best example I could come up with was this one time when I led my Cub Scout troop on a hiking trip. The problem was that didn't exactly end too well. It started out fine, and then I misread my compass, and we got lost in the woods for a couple hours. I decided it was probably best to keep that to myself.

I racked my brain for another example but couldn't think of one worth mentioning. The more time that passed, the more Lauren knew that she had me beat. Eventually, she got bored with watching me struggle and finally put me out of my misery.

"That's exactly what I thought," she said. "You haven't done anything. I, on the other hand, am the point guard on the state champion AAU basketball team and was the sixth-grade vice-president. I'm a proven leader."

"Those are impressive credentials," Noah said.

I noticed Claire begin to nod her head in agreement. I knew that if I didn't act quickly I could be facing an all-out mutiny. And there was no way I could let the recovery of my PlayStation rest in someone else's hands. I needed to compromise.

"Fine! Okay," I said. "How's this? What if you and I run the operation together? Does that work for you?"

I assumed there was a fifty-fifty shot she wouldn't go for it. But that also meant there was a fifty-fifty shot that she would. I guess that's the best thing about fifty-fifty odds.

Lauren rolled her eyes like I was asking the world of her. "I guess," she sighed. "We can run it together."

"Great," I said. "Does that work for the rest of you guys?"

The other cousins nodded in tepid acceptance. Thank God they weren't as hardheaded as Lauren. If it had been a group of Laurens and me, we would have never agreed on anything.

"Cool," I said. "Lauren and I will put together the plan. We'll fill you in as we go. Just remember, if we do this right and work together, no one ever finds out. And our Christmas comes early, instead of not at all."

The cousins all grinned, and so did I. I had every reason to be excited. The ball was officially in motion, and I was one step closer to getting my PlayStation back.

"We'll be in touch," I said as everyone started to leave. I stopped Lauren to talk scheduling. "I'm pretty much free every night this week."

"Shocker," Lauren said. "I have basketball every night."

"Okay . . . well, do you want to just come over to my house afterwards, then?"

"No. You can come to my house afterwards."

"Fine," I said. "Just let me know when to stop by."

"Whatever," Lauren said. She lowered herself out of the tree house and headed on her way.

As I watched her go, I couldn't help but think about how long the next three weeks were gonna be. She just always had to be so difficult. Even with our Christmas presents on the line, she still had to be difficult. The only things certain in life were a pop quiz when you didn't study, your parents saying no to everything, and Lauren being difficult.

I felt a tug on my arm that snapped me from my thoughts and made me jump. Standing beside me was Josh. I'd sworn everyone had already left, but it turned out that the quiet little guy was lingering.

"Is everything okay?" I said.

He didn't say a word. I shook my head: Stupid me for asking. I traced his eyes. They went straight to the Advent calendar. Of course. I had a deal to uphold.

"My bad," I said. I popped a couple chocolates from the tiny calendar windows and handed them to Josh. "There's a couple days of chocolate in advance. Enjoy."

Josh smiled.

I smiled back. "Now get out of here," I said. "I've got a lot of work to do."

To say I had a lot of work to do was a huge understatement. After all, as Benjamin Franklin smartly said, "By failing to prepare, you are preparing to fail."

It actually wouldn't surprise me if he came up with that quote after he got electrocuted while flying his kite in a thunderstorm. Then again, there's a chance that that could have just been what he was preparing to do all along. I mean, he did end up inventing electricity, so I should probably give him the benefit of the doubt, right?

Anyway, I wasn't about to fail. And so, I was determined to prepare more than anyone had ever prepared for anything that had ever been prepared for. I was determined to come up with the ultimate plan.

✿ ✿ ✿

It's a simple fact of life: If you want to be a great baseball player, you study the swing of someone like Bryce Harper; if you want to be a great artist, you study the paintings of any of those guys that the *Teenage Mutant Ninja Turtles* were named after; and if you want to pull off the perfect heist, you study as many of the best heist movies as you can.

My plan to learn from the greats was complicated by the fact that my parents only rarely let me watch even PG-13 movies, and most heist movies were rated R. Luckily, Wes's older brother had a lot of connections and an extensive DVD collection.

The next day at school, I met Wes at his locker to pick up the goods. The stack of movies he handed me was even bigger than I'd been expecting. Included in the pile were *Heat, Ocean's Eleven, Inside Man,* and like ten other classic crime flicks.

"Thanks," I said as I stuffed the DVDs into my backpack.

"Of course," Wes said. "I'm glad to help."

I zipped up my backpack and slung it over my shoulder.

Wes nodded as he looked at me. "You realize that if you guys pull this off, you'll be heroes?"

"If?" I said. "You mean when we pull it off."

"Good. That's the right answer. I like your confidence. You're gonna need to hold onto that."

"Speaking of holding onto things . . . I was thinking, once I have my PlayStation, I'm probably gonna need a place to stash it. And I was thinking your place would be perfect. Since you're parents almost never go down to your basement."

"That more than works for me," Wes said with a grin. "And of course you'll have an open invitation to spend the night anytime you want."

"How does every weekend sound?"

"It sounds great to me." Wes put his fist out for a bump.

I gave Wes a fist bump and then we headed off to class.

🎁 🎁 🎁

After school, I went straight to my room and got to work. I threw *Heat* in my computer's DVD drive and whipped out my school binder for notes.

Just as a warning, anyone under the age of twelve probably shouldn't watch *Heat*. Talk about an intense movie. I won't go into detail about how many nightmares it gave me, but I will say it was less than ten and more than one.

Nightmares aside, there was a really awesome line from it, though. In this great scene, Robert De

Niro tells Al Pacino that you can't get attached to stuff and that you should always be able to walk away from something if you feel heat around the corner. I think heat means the cops and not actual heat, like from a fire or whatever. I'm also pretty sure that was how the movie got its name. Anyway, I thought it was pretty great advice, so I scribbled the quote down in my notes.

After *Heat*, I watched *The Italian Job*. It was probably a better movie to watch for my planning because it wasn't as much about guns as it was about using an even more powerful weapon: your mind. I kept watching movies and taking notes until I got so tired that I actually fell asleep at my desk.

🎁 🎁 🎁

The next day at school, all I could think about was ideas for the plan. When I got home, I went right back to my research.

I'd just finished watching *Ocean's Eleven* when I got a text from Lauren letting me know that she was home and that I should come over.

I threw my notebook in my backpack and headed on my way.

I had one foot out of the front door of my house when I heard my mom call out, "Where do you think you're going?"

I turned to find her and my dad in the living room. They were in the middle of going through our countless boxes of Christmas decorations.

"Out," I said, because it was the first thing that popped in my head and I didn't want to slip up and tell them anything.

"No, you're not," my mom said sternly. "You're grounded."

✦ CHAPTER EIGHT ✦

I WAS GROUNDED? I couldn't believe it. It was news to me. Neither of my parents had mentioned anything about being grounded. And while any grounding—regardless of if it was for two weeks, two months, or two years—would have been a relatively minor sentence when compared to my original punishment, I knew that if I was in fact grounded, so were my plans of getting my PlayStation back. I don't care if you're as skilled as De Niro in *Heat* or Mark Wahlberg in *The Italian Job*, you can't orchestrate a heist from your bedroom.

"What are you talking about?" I shot back, not even trying to hide my anger. "You never told me I was grounded."

"First off, watch your tone with me," my mom said. "And second, I don't need to tell you that you're grounded for you to be grounded."

Talk about classic parent logic. It made absolutely no sense. Even my dad agreed, or at least he tried. "Well, you kinda do at some point," he said before getting cut off by my mom.

"You're not helping," she said to him and then turned her attention back to me. "I'm telling you now. Unless you have something school related, you're not leaving the house."

I must have been subconsciously channeling all one-eighth of my Irish heritage at that moment because I couldn't have been luckier. Just as I was starting to think that I wouldn't be able to work my way out of that jam, my mom had pretty much handed the answer to me on a sleigh-shaped Spode platter.

"It is for school," I said in a much calmer and more agreeable tone. "We have a really big History project, and I was just going to Lauren's to work on it. But you're right, I still shouldn't have spoken to you like I did."

"Who's Lauren?" my mom said, clearly suspicious.

"Lauren Wetterling. My cousin. Your goddaughter."

Looks of confusion swept over both of my parents' faces. They knew how much Lauren and I didn't get along. They couldn't imagine a scenario where we could work together, even if we'd been forced. And that's why it made the whole thing the perfect cover, because they had no reason to doubt that it was actually school related.

"Wait. Seriously?" my dad said.

"Yeah," I said.

"You and Lauren?" my mom said. "Lauren and you?"

"Yes. I can have Aunt Jackie call you when I get there if you don't believe me."

"No . . . I believe you. Just, uh, be back by nine."

"Of course."

I smiled to myself as I left the house. Not only had they bought everything I'd told them, seeing their shock was priceless. I can only imagine the feeling stayed with them for a while, even after I'd left.

I rode my bike to Lauren's house, which was only a mile away. Aunt Jackie was just as stunned as my parents when she answered the front door and heard me say that I was there for Lauren.

When I entered Lauren's room, she was on the phone, gossiping with one of her friends. I scoped out the place while I waited for her to finish her call.

The room was wall-to-wall sports trophies and posters of athletes. Lauren had more athletic accomplishments in real life than I'd won in video games and real life combined, not that I really needed to add the real life part. I touched one of her first-place medals, which got her attention real quick.

"Put that down," Lauren demanded as she hung up her phone. "You're gonna get your greasy fingerprints on it."

"Sorry," I said. "You sure got a lot of medals."

"And I earned every single one of them. Can we just focus on the planning already?" she said, as if it was my fault that we weren't working on the plan.

"Yeah, of course," I said. Her frustration was so convincing that I actually thought it was my fault for a second, until I remembered it totally wasn't. "For the record, I was ready to focus when I got here. You were the one on the phone."

"Well, I'm done now."

"Great. Then let's focus," I said, matching the attitude she was giving me with a little attitude of my own.

Lauren glared at me. She wasn't used to me pushing back so much, but I knew that I had to stand up to her if I wanted to maintain any real say in the operation.

I shrugged my shoulders: What are you waiting for? It seemed to knock her off of the high horse she was on and get her back on track.

"So, I was trying to come up with a plan," she said, "and I realized we might already have a problem. A big one."

"What's that?" I asked, a little worried that she'd discovered something that I'd overlooked.

"Well, if we steal the presents back, won't our parents figure everything out when the donation truck comes to collect and all of them are missing? I mean, our parents aren't that stupid. No one is."

I sighed, relieved. "Don't worry about that. I already took it into consideration. All we gotta do is run a *Due Date*."

"A due date?"

"Yeah. The movie. You didn't see *Due Date*?"

"No, I saw *Due Date*. That's why I'm confused."

"You remember the beginning of the movie, when they accidentally swap suitcases, right?"

"Yeah," she agreed, albeit hesitantly.

"Well, that's exactly what we need to do, but on purpose. We're also gonna need a couple Leon Panettas, a Donatella Versace, and a Mark Zuckerberg. That's at a bare minimum."

Lauren simultaneously shook her head and rolled her eyes.

"What?" I said.

"Do you even know what you're saying?" she asked.

I thought about it for a second, running the plan over in my head one more time. I'd had it right. She clearly hadn't watched *Ocean's Eleven,* or any of the other movies in the Ocean's franchise.

"Yeah, I know what I'm saying," I said. "It's heist terminology. I did a ton of research on pulling scores."

"Scores?"

"That's just more heist lingo. Do you prefer 'jobs'?"

"No. I actually prefer talking like regular kids and not career criminals, since we aren't. But don't let me get in the way of you poorly explaining this whole switching suitcases thing."

"I wasn't talking about switching actual suitcases," I said, trying to defend myself. "It's just code. What we're really gonna do is swap our real presents with decoys. And the rest of what I said was just that we'll need surveillance, a decoy designer, and a tech expert to pull it off."

"Wow!" Lauren said with as much fake enthusiasm as any twelve-year-old girl could possibly muster. "See how much easier that is when you use regular English?"

"Yeah. Sorry," I said as I looked down at my feet. She sure knew how to take the wind out of my sails, or probably anyone's sails. If she'd been on the Santa María with Christopher Columbus, they probably never would've even found America.

What happened next, I definitely didn't see coming. In fact, I never would've guessed it would happen, not in a million years. After a couple seconds of uncomfortable silence—at least for me—Lauren sighed and then mumbled, "No, I'm sorry."

Partly because she hadn't spoken very clearly, but also because what I thought I heard wasn't even close to what I'd been expecting, I could only assume my ears were playing tricks on me. "Wait, what?" I said as I slowly lifted my head.

"I said I'm sorry. Okay?" Lauren said. "You've obviously put a lot of thought into this, and I can respect that."

"Yeah, I have," I said, even more surprised that she said it again. "Apology accepted."

"Good."

We both stood there for a moment. We were in such unfamiliar territory, us being cordial to each other, that neither of us really knew what to say.

I can't speak for Lauren, but I'd even forgotten what we were arguing about.

"So?" Lauren said.

"So?" I said. "What were we even talking about?"

"The plan."

"Oh, yeah, right," I said, regaining my enthusiasm. "We should definitely get back to the plan."

"Yeah," she agreed. "I think your idea is really good and totally solves our problem, but we should probably call it a White Elephant when we explain it to the rest of the cousins. You know, since I doubt most of them have seen *Due Date* and everyone knows about White Elephant."

"That's a great point," I said. "And it's probably even a more fitting title, with the actual gift-swap and all."

"Exactly. We're switching out the bad for the good. So, do you have any more ideas?"

"Actually, I think I have it pretty much all mapped out."

"Well then, let me know how we're gonna pull this score."

I couldn't help but chuckle at her using the lingo.

"What?" Lauren said, self-conscious. "Did I use that right?"

"Yeah, that was right," I said with a grin. "Oh, and before I forget, I told my parents that we're working on a History project. You should probably tell your parents the same so our stories match."

"Good thinking. I will. Now hit me with the details of the score."

I laid out the rest of the plan to Lauren and then we spent the next couple hours working together to figure out the most efficient way to execute it. We both agreed that making the decoys should be the first task, since that was definitely gonna take the longest. Before we wrapped up our meeting, we contacted the rest of the cousins and let them in on their first tasks: they all needed to re-create their Christmas lists and find out what wrapping paper their parents had used.

As I left Lauren's house, I couldn't help but be surprised at how well we'd been able to work together—not counting the little hiccup at the beginning, of course. It turned out we actually made a pretty solid team when we wanted to. While we still had a long way to go, we were at least moving in the right direction, and things were only about to start moving even faster.

❆ CHAPTER NINE ❆

THE NEXT DAY after school, my dad asked me if I wanted to go on the roof with him to set up the Christmas lights. Like most kids, I'd been trying to get my dad to let me go on the roof with him for years, but he always maintained that it was too dangerous. Instead, he would make me stand by the ladder and feed him the lights. But now . . . he was practically begging me to join him.

"Come on," he insisted. "It'll be fun."

The surprise offer threw me for such a loop that I almost said yes right on the spot. Thankfully, I was able to restrain myself. I could tell by his enthusiasm that he clearly had ulterior motives. Ever since I'd turned down the Christmas pageant, I'd noticed that my parents were acting a little different.

While the hunger strike and vow of silence hadn't moved them, they were clearly concerned about the possibility of an all-out Christmas boycott. My dad might've thought he could buy me, but I wasn't for sale. I decided that if a Christmas boycott was what they feared, a Christmas boycott was what they'd get.

"What's the point?" I said, and shrugged my shoulders. "They're just gonna come down in a couple weeks anyway. Besides, I got slammed with homework today."

"Oh," my dad said, his shoulders slumping.

"Maybe next year though," I said.

I couldn't help but feel a little bit bad for the guy as I watched him head outside by himself. However, I quickly overcame that feeling by reminding myself of my seized PlayStation and his passive acceptance of my punishment.

I waited for a couple minutes after my dad left and then went to check on my mom in the kitchen. She was in the middle of making dinner. I knew that would probably keep her attention until it was time to eat, since she didn't like to leave the kitchen with the stove on. With both of my parents preoccupied, it was time to make my move and find the wrapping paper.

I had Connor stand guard at the bottom of the stairs, just to be safe, and then sneaked into my parents' room.

The first thing I did was check under the bed. I wasn't expecting to find any wrapping paper; I just wanted to see if the PlayStation was still there. It wasn't. They'd already moved it. Most likely it was now hidden under the bed at my grandparents' house, or wherever they hid their presents.

I didn't let my disappointment distract me; there wasn't time for that. I had a job to do. I quickly returned my focus to my wrapping paper search.

Searching for wrapping paper is a lot easier than searching for presents since there's no real reason to hide it. Most of the time, my parents would just leave it out in plain sight, and I'd find out what paper they'd picked without even trying to. Of course, Murphy's Law—no relation to me, as far as I know—that whatever can go wrong will go wrong, likes to rear its annoying head in a lot of situations that are supposed to be easy, and this situation was no exception. I scanned the room three times and didn't spot even a single roll of wrapping paper.

It doesn't make much sense now, but at that time I figured that they had to have hidden the rolls. I checked all of the same logical hiding spots I'd dug through the previous time I scoured the room, but they were just as fruitless as they'd been before. I began to pace, splitting my thoughts between trying to come up with ideas and doubting whether I'd ever find it.

I'd made a couple laps back and forth when the answer finally hit me: scraps, not rolls. I shouldn't have been looking for rolls. The presents were gone, which meant that they were wrapped. That meant the rolls were already used and all that would be left were scraps.

I rushed to the trashcan that was next to my parents' bed and dug through the contents. Resting at the bottom of the tiny pile of garbage were a couple pieces of wrapping paper. Jackpot! I pocketed a small section of the unused paper and slipped out of the bedroom undetected.

🎁 🎁 🎁

After dinner, Connor and I went straight to my room to re-create our Christmas lists. Connor rattled off all of the presents he'd asked for. I swear it took at least ten minutes to get them all down.

"Is that it?" I said sarcastically as I finished writing the last gift from his seemingly never-ending list.

"I think so," Connor said.

"Okay, I—"

"Wait!" Connor cut me off. He paused and then took a deep breath before sheepishly adding, "I forgot one."

"Okay. What is it?"

Connor didn't respond. He just looked away.

I tapped the pen on the paper as I waited for his answer. "You know I'm not gonna be able to put it on the list if you don't tell me, right?" But Connor still wouldn't answer. "Come on. You already told Santa. You can tell me."

"Fine," he said. "I asked for a Dream Lite Pillow Pet."

"Aren't you a little old for that?"

"No. You didn't like the dark when your were my age."

He had a point. Even at that time, I didn't like the dark. Truthfully, I still don't. I probably never will. I mean, if those pillows came in sports teams or anything other than stuffed animals, I could maybe get behind asking for one. Don't judge me.

"You're right," I said.

"See. Just put it down."

I added the Pillow Pet to Connor's list.

"Time to write your list," Connor said.

I made a section for my wish list. In big, bold letters I wrote the only thing that I'd put on my Christmas wish list: SONY PLAYSTATION 4. I underlined it three times for emphasis.

"That's it?" Connor said. "Just one thing?"

"It's a PlayStation 4," I said. "Once I have it, what else could I possibly need?"

"Games?"

"Good point. Might as well make a couple decoy games." I added a few games to my list. "That's it. Now go get your piggy bank."

"Why do you need my piggy bank?"

"For the money inside it. Building the decoys and pulling off this heist is gonna cost money. To fund it, we're gonna need to pool our resources."

"Okay," Connor said, and then ran off to grab his money.

🎁　🎁　🎁

It took a few days for Lauren and me to round up all of the lists and money. Not everyone was eager to contribute their savings. Lauren really had to lean on Ryan to get him to fork over all of the money he'd hoarded. He argued that since his allowance was higher and he'd spent more years working, he'd have to pay more for his presents than everyone else.

I didn't disagree with his logic, but we really needed his funds, so I told Lauren to just push harder. She did, and eventually he caved. She said he made her wait in the doorway with her back turned so she didn't see his hiding spots. She also said he complained the whole time too.

Once Lauren and I had gathered everything, we consolidated what we'd collected and headed to Claire's house.

Claire lived in the really nice area my mom liked to call the McMansions. She never told me what she called our neighborhood, but the McNuggets seems fitting.

Claire's room was ridiculous. Besides being four times the size of my room, it was set up like a mini clothing designer's workshop. There were mannequins, huge spools of fabric, and all sorts of other weird things that fashion people are into.

"You're gonna need to use all your design skills to create the decoys," Lauren said as she handed the wrapping paper samples and Christmas lists to Claire.

"Don't worry," Claire said, "they'll look better than the real—"

Claire went silent as she was interrupted by a knock at the bedroom door. Her eyes grew wide.

"It's okay," I said. "I'm pretty sure I know who that is, and it's not your mom." I opened the door. Waiting in the hallway was Noah.

"Good afternoon, teammates," he said with a smile and then entered the room. "Sorry I'm late."

Claire glared at me. "Excuse me. What is he doing here?"

"He's here to help," I said. "We know that you can make the fake presents look just like the real ones, but they also gotta feel like the real presents. That's where Noah comes in."

"Please tell me you're J.K. Rowling."

"We're not just kidding," Lauren said. "His engineering and math expertise will make sure the decoys pass for the real presents in every way possible."

"And they will," Noah said.

"Good."

"I will see to it that no present leaves this room until it satisfies all of the necessary tests. Including but not limited to the size test, the weight test, and, most importantly, the shake test."

"I want to give you the shake test," Claire said.

"That would not do us any good. Now, if you do not mind, may I examine the list?" Noah said as he reached for the list.

Claire yanked it away from his outstretched hand. "Just give me a second." She looked over the list, shook her head, and chuckled. "A telescope? You can't be for reals. What are you gonna do with that, look at the stars?"

"Yes," Noah said. "That is precisely what they are for."

"OMG. You're such a nerd."

I could tell Noah's feelings were getting hurt and that I needed to step in and be a leader. "Listen," I said, "it's perfectly all right if you guys aren't best buddies, but you're gonna need to work together. Just look at Lauren and I. We don't like each other at all. But if we can work together, so can you. Right, Lauren?"

I turned to Lauren for backup. But she was stuck in her own thoughts and didn't respond. "Right, Lauren?" I repeated, finally getting her attention.

"Oh, yeah," she agreed. "He's right. About both parts."

"Fine," Claire said. She handed Noah the list.

I gave Claire the wad of money that we'd collected. "That should cover your expenses. But it's all the money we have, so make sure you spend it wisely."

"Perf. I will," Claire said. "I mean, we will."

"Great," I said. "We'll check in on you guys later."

I followed Lauren out of the room and then shut the door behind us.

"Do you think they're gonna be okay working together?" Lauren asked.

"I have no idea," I said. "But for the sake of the heist, they better be."

"Yeah. So what's next on our list?"

"Task two: security. We need to know what we're up against. And we need to figure out how we're gonna get inside to pull off the switch."

🎁 🎁 🎁

When it comes to home security, there are basically two types of old people. The first type is the clueless kind. They still think they live in the olden days, when everyone in the neighborhood was best friends and baked each other apple pies. They honestly believe that every spam email they ever get is actually from a Nigerian prince with tons of money for them, and they almost never lock their doors or windows. The other type is the "get off my lawn" kind of old people. They're the opposite of clueless. They're overly protective and even get suspicious when a Girl Scout they don't recognize tries to sell them Thin Mints.

My grandparents' front door was almost always unlocked whenever we'd go over, so I was crossing my fingers that they fell into the clueless camp.

Of course, I knew that the only way that we could find out for sure would be by performing a full-scale security check. Lauren suggested that Ryan would be the best person for the job. Apparently, he'd been sneaking out of their house for years and hadn't been caught yet. The fact that he hadn't been busted obviously meant that he wasn't just good at sneaking out, but that he was also skilled at sneaking back in.

Ryan said he'd need a couple days to pull off his security check. He wanted to make sure that he covered every base, and he claimed there were a lot of bases. I wouldn't have known; I'd only ever tried to sneak out of the front door during the day and had been busted every time.

🎁 🎁 🎁

While Ryan worked on identifying any security issues, Lauren and I got a jump on our third task: transportation.

Transportation for any kid under the age of sixteen, and even some unfortunate kids over sixteen, almost always means relying on your parents for a ride. But it wasn't like we could just ask my dad or some random adult to be the wheelman on our job. That wouldn't fly. So, given our situation, we needed to look elsewhere.

The next day at school, I put out some feelers and was able to find a hookup. A classmate's father happened to run the biggest bicycle and bicycle accessory shop in the area, and he said that he "had us covered."

After school, Lauren and I headed to the nearby mall where the shop was located. The mall was packed. Holiday shoppers were out in droves. We cut through the crowd until we arrived at our destination: Bill's Bikes.

The welcome bell rang as we entered the store.

Our hookup, Floyd Bailey, was waiting behind the front counter with his dad, the Bill of Bill's Bikes. Floyd was small for his age and suffered from severe, early-onset Napoleon complex. He was as fiery as the orange hair on his head and was one of the angriest and, consequently, one of the least liked kids in our entire middle school.

I waved to Floyd. He winked and then gestured to the corner of the store, where they kept all of the bike strollers.

Lauren and I met Floyd in the corner.

"So . . . you like anything you see?" Floyd asked.

"Of course. I like it all," I said. I pointed at the biggest covered two-seater they had in stock. "But I especially like that one. It's exactly what I was imagining."

"Then it looks like today's your lucky day. My dad has three of these babies at our house," Floyd said as he ran his hand across the stroller I'd selected.

Lauren nodded her head. "Three of those should be more than enough cargo space to fit all of our presents in one trip."

"Yeah," I agreed. "Thanks, Floyd."

"Excuse me," Floyd snapped. "What did you call me?"

I'd totally forgotten about one of the other reasons people didn't like Floyd: He'd actually made up his own nickname. He had this side business of lending kids at school money, and he insisted that everyone call him Shark or "The Shark," which I guess was short for loan shark. No one ever really did, except for the kids who were so desperate for a bag of chips or something else from the vending machines that they put up with him—and the 100 percent interest he charged.

"Sorry, Shark," I said. "That was my bad."

"Yes, it was," he smugly agreed.

"It won't happen again," I said even more apologetically. "Anyway, we really appreciate you giving us the strollers to use." I offered my hand, so we could seal the deal with a shake.

"You can put that hand back in your pocket, partner," Floyd said. "We're not shaking on anything just yet. There's still a lot to discuss. First and foremost, we still need to talk price."

"Uh, what do you mean?" I said, confused. "You told me you had us covered."

"Yes, I did. And yes, I do," he said. "I'll have these ready for you when you need them. I'm even more than happy to give you the friend price, even though you two don't really treat me like a friend that often, if ever. But just because I said that I had you covered, doesn't mean you're getting something for nothing. This isn't Communist Russia."

"But we don't have any more money," Lauren said. "We're all tapped out."

"I don't know what to tell you," Floyd said with a shrug. "That sounds like more of a 'you' problem than a 'me' problem. You can come back when you have the coin. But for now, this meeting is over." He turned and started back toward the front counter.

⚜ CHAPTER TEN ⚜

FLOYD WAS RIGHT. It's was definitely more of a "you" problem, or a "we" problem, and not getting the strollers would've been an even bigger "we" problem. Sure, there was a chance we'd be able to pull off the heist without them, but it would significantly increase the amount of time it took to pull the whole thing off, which would increase our chances of getting caught. Without the strollers, we'd really be putting ourselves up against the wall. We couldn't risk it. And while it's clearly a good sign that you're up to no good when you're forced to negotiate with "no good" people, that's exactly what we had to do.

"Wait," I begged, stopping Floyd in his tracks. "There's gotta be a way we can make this work."

Floyd turned back around, a devious grin draped on his face. "There might be a way. But it's gonna cost you. And I'm talking quarters on the dollar."

"We already told you we don't have any more money," Lauren said.

"I'm not talking about money," Floyd said. "I'm talking about trade."

"What kinda trade?" I asked.

"All I want," Floyd said, his grin growing, "is what you don't want. I'm talking about socks, sweaters, you name it. Anything from your Christmas list that you don't want, I do."

"Why do you want that crap?" Lauren said.

"I have my reasons."

Lauren shot Floyd one of her all-too-familiar icy stares. I never thought I could be happy to see that look from her, but it wasn't pointed at me, so I was actually able to enjoy it. I also enjoyed watching Floyd crack like an egg.

Floyd swallowed hard. "I have a fence," he said, his voice squeaking.

"So do I," Lauren said, "only I don't dress mine up in socks and sweaters."

"He doesn't mean a yard fence," I said. "He means a buyer."

"Oh."

"Look at you, Murphy," Floyd said as he nodded his head. "You really know your stuff. I'm impressed. Anyway, my guy specializes in unwanted Christmas presents. I usually get 25 percent of the retail price. It's not much, but it gives me a little extra capital. And that's just from my gifts, which isn't much. But if we're talking seven kids' unwanted presents—there's seven of you, right?"

"Yeah," I said.

"With seven kids' unwanted presents, that could add up real quick. I should be able to make my fee."

"I think that's reasonable enough," I said. I turned to Lauren to see if she was on board.

"That's fine with me," she said. "As long as WE decide what we don't want. Not you."

"Like I said, YOU name it," Floyd said. He offered his hand to close the deal.

I returned the favor and gave it a shake. I should have seen it coming, but he squeezed my hand as hard as he could. I know people say a firm handshake makes you seem confident, but there's a fine line between being confident and being a jerk. I'm not the strongest guy in the world. I wasn't even the strongest person in the room—Lauren had me beat—but I was stronger than Floyd, and I let him know it. I squeezed his hand as hard as I could.

"Easy!" Floyd yelped, wincing. He yanked his hand free and then attempted to shake the sting out of it.

"Are we good?" I asked.

"Yeah. Just let me know when you guys lock down a date."

"We will," I said. "We've got our people working on it."

We didn't actually have "our people" on it—not yet, at least. However, it was the next thing on our list. And to figure out the date, we needed to implement our fourth task: reconnaissance.

🎁 🎁 🎁

"What does that even mean?" Connor asked after we told him that he would be in charge of pulling reconnaissance.

A couple days had passed since our dealings with Floyd—scheduling and school stuff had slowed us down—but Lauren and I were finally able to meet up with Connor and Josh in my tree house to discuss their mission.

Connor stared at me with complete bewilderment while I tried to come up with an explanation he could understand. There are few things harder than trying to define a word that you hardly know the definition for.

"It means . . . reconnaissance," I said.

"Great," Connor said. "That helps a lot."

"It means you and Josh get to hang out with Grandma and Grandpa," Lauren said. "But you aren't just hanging out for fun. You need to watch what they do and find out everything you can about them."

"Yeah," I said. "That's what I was trying to say. We need to know everything. We need to know when they wake up. When they go to sleep. How they take their coffee. Or if they even like coffee. Maybe they don't like coffee."

"I already know they like coffee," Lauren said.

"Good," I said. "We know they like coffee. You guys don't need to find that out. You just need to find out everything else."

"Sounds easy enough," Connor said.

"It is easy," Lauren said. "That's why we gave you the job."

"But it's also really important," I added. "Because you're gonna need to find out when Grandma and Grandpa are gonna be out of the house. That's the only time it will be safe for us to go in and steal our presents back."

Connor turned to Josh. They shared a nod. He turned back to Lauren and me, full of six-year-old bravado. "You can count on us," he said.

"Perfect," I said. "There's just one more thing before you guys go." I popped a week's worth of chocolates from the Advent calendar and handed them to Josh. "Now, that's a lot of chocolate, so you might want to—"

Before I could finish, Josh threw all of the chocolates into his mouth. He grinned as much as his full cheeks would let him.

"That works too," I said. "Enjoy."

Josh and Connor climbed out of the tree house and headed off on their mission.

"Should we go check in on Claire and Noah?" I asked Lauren, who was reading a message on her cell phone.

"I have a better idea," she said as she finished reading. "Ryan said he's done with his security check and that he'll be back at my house in ten minutes."

🎁 🎁 🎁

Lauren and I biked as fast as we could to her house. Once there, we met up with Ryan, who was waiting in his room.

"I was this close to getting busted," Ryan said, holding his fingers millimeters apart to illustrate how close it had been.

"But you didn't, right?" I said.

"Of course not. Then it would have been this close." He squeezed his fingers together so that they touched. "And I also probably wouldn't be here if I had."

"What happened?" Lauren asked.

"I was pulling my night watch last night," Ryan said, "and hiding in the bushes when, out of nowhere, this massive Rottweiler comes growling and snarling toward me. I was sure I was gonna be Puppy Chow. Thankfully, his owner yanked him away at the last second."

"Did you see the owner?" I said.

"Yeah," Ryan said. "It was the guy who lives at the end of Grandma and Grandpa's street."

"Mr. Barker?" I said.

"I don't know his name, but that sounds right."

"He doesn't have a Rottweiler," Lauren said.

"Yeah," I agreed. "It's the nicest black Lab ever."

"Hey, I'm not a dog expert," Ryan said, getting defensive. "And it was dark. But I swear it growled and was trying to bite me."

"It was probably trying to lick you," Lauren said.

"Well, whatever it was trying to do, it made me fall in the bushes, which is how I got all these scratches." Ryan held out his arms to display the evidence: a dozen or more intersecting gashes.

"Ouch," I said. The cuts definitely looked painful.

"Yep," Ryan said, "those didn't exactly tickle."

"So what did you learn from your near-death encounter in the bushes?" Lauren asked.

"That Grandma and Grandpa live on a higher traffic street than we do," Ryan said. "There were cars passing every ten to fifteen seconds. Lots of late-night joggers and dog walkers too. Given the tight window and our varying levels of skill, the odds that we can make it in the front without getting spotted are slim to none."

"So going in the front isn't an option?" I said.

"Not in my mind," Ryan said.

"Well, what about the back door?" Lauren said.

"That has obstacles of its own," Ryan said. "I had to fake like I wanted to do yard work to get close to everything, but I found this." He pulled out his phone and flipped through the pics he'd taken of our grandparents' house. Each corner of the house had a different motion detector light.

"They look pretty old," I said, pointing to the rust forming around some of the detectors.

"They are," Ryan said. "That's one of the things we have going for us. Most new motion detectors have a coverage area of 180 degrees, but the lights Grandpa has only cover 90 degrees. The other thing we have going for us is that my dad actually helped Grandpa install them, and in spite of what he thinks, he isn't the handiest guy around."

"That's definitely true," Lauren agreed.

"Yeah," Ryan said. "I could be wrong, but I think there might be two gaps in the coverage zones. I put together a little mock-up." He retrieved a sheet of paper from his pocket.

It was a sketch of our grandparents' house and yard. All of the motion detectors were identified, along with their expected coverage areas, which were shaded.

"Here and here are the potential gaps," Ryan said as he pointed to the two spots that had been left unshaded.

"Wow," I said, impressed. "You really are good."

"Thanks," Ryan said. "But that's not even the best part. The best part is where those spots lead. The first one leads to the area under the second story bathroom. The other one gives us a diagonal path right to the back door."

"No way," I said. "That has to be the worst installation job anyone has ever done."

"Seriously," Lauren said. "I mean, it's good for us, but it's just really bad. Like, someone should probably tell Grandpa about that."

"Definitely," I said. "But only after we get our presents back."

"Yeah. Of course."

"Don't get too excited just yet," Ryan said. "I still gotta go back sometime when Grandma and Grandpa aren't around or are busy to confirm that the gaps are real and mark them off."

"Okay," I said. "We can easily make that happen."

"But even if I'm right, there's still a much bigger obstacle."

"What's that?" Lauren asked.

"The back door," Ryan said, gravely.

"That shouldn't be a problem," I said. "I'm pretty sure my mom has the key."

"She probably does," Ryan said. "So does our mom. And while the key will help us with the deadbolt, what worries me is the chain lock."

"I didn't even know they had one," I said. I'd never even gone in or out the back door, just the front.

"Me either," Ryan said, almost disappointed in himself for never noticing it before.

"Is it like the one we have at our house?" Lauren said.

"Pretty close to the same," Ryan said. "But the big difference is that Grandpa actually uses his.

He has total OCD about it too. He checks it all the time, especially before he leaves the house. I tried to stay back and unlock it once, but he wouldn't leave without me leaving first, and then he just went back and relocked it. The same thing goes for all of the windows."

So much for hoping that our grandparents fell into the first group of old people. Nope, they were in their own third group, a hybrid of the two, clueless at home and careful when gone.

"Do you have any ideas for how we can get around it?" I asked, hoping for good news.

"Unfortunately, I don't," Ryan said. "And to be brutally honest, if we don't come up with something, I don't see how we get inside."

⚜ CHAPTER ELEVEN ⚜

LAUREN AND I met up after school for a whole week trying to come up with a way to bypass the chain lock. With only eight days left until Christmas, we still weren't any closer to coming up with a solution than we'd been when we started. The reality that we might not find a way inside our grandparents' house was setting in, and with that realization came frustration.

I paced back and forth in Lauren's room while she lounged on her bed, tossing a basketball in the air. "You realize this probably isn't the best time to work on your shot," I said.

"I don't need to work on my shot," Lauren snapped back. "I'm doing this because it helps me think. I assumed that's why you were walking all over the place, and not because you were trying to burn calories or something."

"Sorry. I didn't mean to come off so harsh," I said. "The fact that we're running out of time is really getting to me."

"Yeah, well, it's getting to me too. So is the fact that every idea we come up with doesn't work."

"There's gotta be something. We just haven't thought of it—" I stopped myself, both words and walking. I was pretty sure I had the perfect idea.

"What?" Lauren said, probably noticing the twinkle in my eye. "Do you have an idea?"

"Oh, yeah," I said. "Our problem is that we keep thinking about how we can get from the outside in, when we should be going from the inside out."

"You lost me on that."

"We can totally bypass the lock by running an inside man," I said.

"Why does it gotta be an inside MAN?" Lauren asked, clearly offended. "Why can't it be an inside woman?"

"It totally can be. That's just the name of the movie."

"Oh," she said, calming down. "I never saw *Inside Man.*"

"It's a good one," I said. "Denzel is great in it.

But I can tell you more about it later. Anyway, the move is basically what it sounds like. All we gotta to do is get someone, man or woman, on the inside."

"You mean like bribing Grandma or Grandpa?"

"No. This is a lot easier."

"Good. 'Cause I don't think that would actually be easy."

"Me either, but this is. On the morning of the heist, a few of us go to Grandma and Grandpa's house and just hang out. After a while, all of us leave, except for the inside person, who stays behind and hides out."

"For the whole day?" Lauren asked.

"Not the whole day, but maybe most of it."

"Not to poke holes in this plan, but what if they get hungry?"

"We can pack them a lunch. Drinks. Snacks. Whatever."

"What about when they gotta go to the bathroom?"

I thought about it for a second before finally remembering, "I think Denzel wore a diaper in the movie. Either that or he used a jug."

"You can't be serious."

"Desperate times call for desperate measures," I said. After all, we were well beyond the point of being desperate.

"So you're volunteering for that?"

"Sure."

"Here's the thing," Lauren said. "Even if you packed a lunch and wore a diaper, there still isn't a good place to hide. Every closet and storage space is packed with junk. Ryan and I tried to play hide-and-seek at their house a couple years ago and it's basically impossible. Unless you want to spend the day in their creepy unfinished basement."

The thought alone gave me chills. I'd rather wear a diaper to school for a week than spend thirty minutes by myself in that basement. My face must have shown what I was thinking because all Lauren said was, "Exactly."

"I couldn't ask anyone to go through that," I said.

"Me either," Lauren agreed.

"Then I guess we're back at square one," I said, and then plopped down in Lauren's desk chair.

"More like square negative one."

"Yeah," I sulked. "My mom says that when you're trying to find something, it's always in the last place you look."

"Of course it is," Lauren said. "Why would you keep looking after you've found what you're looking for?"

"That is a good point." It really was. I'd never actually thought about it like that, but seriously, why would someone keep looking? I guess not all sayings make sense.

"My mom always says everything happens when you least expect it," Lauren said.

"Does that mean we should stop trying to think of an answer or expecting to find one?"

"Honestly, I don't know. Maybe?"

"What should we do while we aren't thinking of answers?"

"Beats me," Lauren said. She thought about it for a second. "I'm gonna grab a drink. You want something?"

"Sure," I said.

We headed to the kitchen and grabbed a couple sodas from the fridge. All they had was diet cola, so I didn't have much of a choice.

"Diet cola is easily the worst of the diet drinks," I said.

Lauren made a face as if I'd personally attacked her, like I'd criticized her shooting form or something else she held dear. "What are you talking about?" she said.

"What am I talking about? It tastes nothing like regular cola. Diet Dr. Pepper, on the other hand?

Now that's a real diet soda."

"Who said the goal of a diet soda was to taste like the original?"

"I don't know. Shouldn't it be?" I threw my hands up and shrugged my shoulders. When I did, I accidentally brushed against the fridge door, knocking a couple of Aunt Jackie's holiday themed refrigerator magnets to the ground.

One of the magnets popped from its figurine on impact.

"Sorry about that," I said. "I can fix it."

"Don't worry about it," Lauren said as she picked up the broken magnet. "My mom has so many of these, she probably won't even notice."

I watched as the loose magnet flipped in Lauren's hand. It sparked an idea in my brain. "Magnets!" I blurted out.

"Yeah, they're magnets," Lauren said while giving me a look like I'd just said the dumbest and most obvious thing ever.

"No. I mean, of course they're magnets. But what I really meant is that I just had an idea for the chain lock. Watch this." I grabbed the magnets from her hand and used the nearby basement door to demonstrate what I was thinking. I placed the broken magnet and the intact figurine on opposites sides of the door. The magnetic attraction held the two in place.

"If we can plant a magnet on the back of the chain lock," I said, "we can use a second to slide the lock into the unlocked position." I moved the magnets on the backside of the door and the figurine moved correspondingly.

"Okay," Lauren said. "Then how do we get the lock out?"

"Simple," I said. "We flip the outside magnet around. That switches the polarity. North attracts south, but north repels north." I held the two magnets together, matching their poles. The top magnet shot away, spun, and then attached to the bottom magnet. "That will pop the lock out, and then we'll pop in."

"Oh my god. That's genius," Lauren said. She shook me by my shoulders. "You're a genius!"

"I don't know about that," I said with a grin, "but it is a good idea."

"It's a great idea. Now we just need to talk to your brother and Josh and see what they've learned."

My smile vanished as I realized, "Oh, crap. I totally forgot they were still on their recon. We definitely need to pull them out of the field. They're probably dying right now."

The next day, Lauren and I met with Connor and Josh in my tree house. The tree house was becoming less practical as a meeting spot with the colder weather settling in. To remedy that, I borrowed my dad's garage space heater, which I hooked up using one of his super-long extension cords.

"We're so sorry we forgot about you guys," I said. "We just got caught up trying to solve a huge problem."

"No biggie," Connor said. "We actually had a lot of fun hanging out with Grandma and Grandpa."

Josh smiled and nodded in agreement.

"That's great," Lauren said. "What did you guys find out?"

"Before we get to that," Connor said, "you guys owe Josh a lot of chocolate."

"Right, sorry," I said. I retrieved the Advent calendar from my backpack, popped a week's worth of chocolates, and handed them to Josh. "There you go."

"Now tell us everything you learned," Lauren said.

"Where do I start?" Connor said. "Grandma and Grandpa are like a couple of preschoolers. All their activities are totally planned. Every day, they wake up at 5:30 in the morning and eat breakfast.

I asked Grandpa what they eat, and he just said, 'Too much fiber.' Whatever that means."

"What do they do after breakfast?" I said.

"They watch some TV show about a radio show," Connor said. "I think it's called Amos or Imus. Whatever it's called, it should be called boring because that's what it really is. Once that's over, they watch the news until 1 p.m."

"What happens then?" Lauren said.

"Grandma makes lunch," Connor said. "Usually a sandwich or some leftovers. After lunch, they watch cooking shows until 7 p.m., when Grandpa goes upstairs. He told us that he was 'going to take the Browns to the Super Bowl,' but I think he really just goes to the bathroom. And I'm pretty sure it's a 'number two,' because Grandma always tells him to remember to crack the window."

"I think you're probably right about that," I said.

"Grandpa also goes 'number one' a lot," Connor said. "He said it's because his prostate is a grapefruit, or the size of a grapefruit, or something like that."

"Okay, great," Lauren said. "I think we can move past all the bodily functions stuff."

"Excuse me," Connor said. "You guys told me that you wanted to know everything."

"You're right. We did," I said. "What else did you learn?"

"They have dinner at 7:30," Connor said. "Then they watch the news and argue with the TV until they go to sleep at ten. The next day, they wake up and do the same exact thing."

"Did they mention anything about leaving the house?" I asked.

"Only that they don't like to," Connor said. "They do go to church and the grocery store every Sunday morning, but that's about it."

"That doesn't work. We can't pull this off in the morning. They don't do any kind of date night like Mom and Dad do?"

Connor shook his head.

I was still trying to come up with a solution when Lauren snapped her fingers.

"Church! That's it!" Lauren said. "They don't just go on Sunday morning. They went to the Christmas Eve Mass last year. Remember, we all did."

"Yeah," I said, "but that was only because I was in the kids' Christmas pageant. I'm not doing that this year."

"Dang. You're right," Lauren said. "And we can't afford to have you be a decoy just to get them out of the house. We need you for the heist."

No sooner had Lauren finished speaking than she and I shared the same realization. We both turned to Connor.

"I think you're thinking what I'm thinking," I said.

"I think I'm thinking it too," Lauren said.

"Hey," Connor whined. "Why are you guys looking at me like that?"

A slight grin crossed Lauren's face. "It looks like we got a new task five."

"Yes, it does," I said, my own smile matching hers.

Ben Franklin didn't specifically mention what his preparing entailed, but I think if he'd been asked for a list, one of the things he would have definitely included in his preparation would be preparing for change. After all, you can only really control what you can control, and there's way more that you can't. That's why the best plans are written in pencil and not pen. That way, they can always be rewritten depending on the circumstances.

While we'd initially had one idea of how everything was gonna go down, it was clear that we needed to deviate slightly from our original plans. We needed a diversion to get our grandparents out of their house. Thankfully, we had the perfect idea for how we could pull that off.

♣ CHAPTER TWELVE ♣

THE NEXT EVENING, our parents didn't even ask Connor and me if we wanted to go with them to the tree farm to pick out our Christmas tree. We'd already turned down their invitation to drive around and look at lights, and also squashed their idea of going to our local Christmas parade. They were pretty distraught after the last one, which is probably why they decided it was easier to just go grab a tree without asking us to join them.

With just Connor and me left home alone, I used the opportunity to prep him on how to handle our parents. While I had a feeling that our parents' emotionally heightened state might cloud their judgment and ability to see that they were being played, I knew that believability was still gonna be a very important part of making sure the diversion would work. Plus, like Benny Franklin said, you gotta prepare.

🎁 🎁 🎁

My mom and dad returned home shortly after I'd finished prepping Connor. They set up the tree in the living room and then started stringing popcorn to wrap around the branches.

Ever since I'd learned how to make popcorn garland in preschool, it'd been our tradition to cover the tree in garlands as soon as we got home from the tree farm. We combined that tradition with my dad's childhood custom of not putting the rest of the ornaments on the tree until Christmas Eve. Of course, I had no intention of taking part in either phase of decorating.

I quietly crept down the stairs with Connor. I wanted to make sure I could hear everything that went down. That way, if things got out of control, I could always barge in and save him. I stayed hidden behind the wall in the stairway while Connor continued down the last couple steps and strolled into the living room.

"Hey, big guy," my dad said cheerfully as Connor entered. "Did you come to help us with the tree?"

"No," Connor said. "I'm actually really slammed with schoolwork."

I'd given him that line. It was my go-to excuse whenever my parents asked me to do something I didn't want to do. In hindsight, I probably should have given him a different verb than "slammed," maybe something like "crushed" or "bombarded," so it would've been less obvious that he'd been coached. Fortunately, my parents didn't even notice.

"Oh," my dad said, clearly disappointed.

"Yeah," Connor continued. "I was just wondering if it's too late to get in the Christmas pageant?"

"What? Really? Why?" my mom said, tripping over her words.

"I don't know," Connor said. "I think it could be fun."

"It would definitely be lots of fun," my mom squealed, unable to contain her excitement. "I mean, all of the big roles are most likely already taken, but Mrs. Johnston usually has a whole flock of sheep. I don't see why she couldn't have another."

"I don't need to be the star. I'll take what I can get."

"Great!" my mom said. "I'll talk to her first thing tomorrow."

As proof that my parents couldn't see what was going on, my poor dad misjudged the situation and overplayed his hand. "Speaking of talking to people, Connor," he said, "do you want to go to the mall sometime and have a little chat with Santa?"

"What's the point?" Connor said. "We're not getting presents. What am I gonna talk to Santa about, the weather?" When he said that, I was smiling on the inside and the outside. I hadn't given him that line, but it was a great one. I could only imagine the looks on my parents' faces.

"Well. I mean," my dad struggled to come up with a response. "You could always talk about next year or something."

"If I need to tell Santa anything, I'll just send him an email," Connor said. "Mom knows what I'm talking about."

As Connor left the room, I heard my mom whisper, "I have no idea what he's talking about."

I greeted Connor with a closed fist. He gave me a bump.

"Great job, buddy," I whispered. I threw my arm around his shoulder and squeezed him tight as we headed back up the stairs.

🎁 🎁 🎁

The next day, all of the cousins met up at Claire's house. Everyone sat in a circle as I brought them up to speed.

"Not only is Connor in the pageant, but Grandma and Grandpa already told my mom they'll be there," I said. "That means the date is set. We're going in on Christmas Eve, just before the donation truck. It's a tight window, but we'll make it work."

Smiles crept across all of their faces. You could feel the excitement fill up the room.

"I guess that means Christmas Eve is our Christmas," Ryan said.

"And the eve of Christmas Eve is our Christmas Eve," Noah added.

"Yes, it does," I said. "It also means that we got less than five days to finish making the decoys. That's why we're all here. Everyone needs to pitch in so we can make sure all of the presents are ready." I nodded to Claire and Noah. "They're all yours."

They both hopped up from the floor and took center stage.

"There's a right way and a wrong way to wrap presents," Claire said and then turned to Noah to let him speak.

"We are going to teach you the right way," Noah said.

"Follow us."

Lauren and I stayed back while Claire led the rest of the cousins to her makeshift wrapping station.

"We still gotta plant the magnet," Lauren said.

"I know," I said. "I was thinking we could cook Grandma and Grandpa a little dinner and do it then. That'll also give us a chance to execute the final task left before pulling off the heist."

"Task six," Lauren said. "Visual confirmation."

I smiled and nodded.

🎁 🎁 🎁

Lauren arranged for us to make dinner for our grandparents a couple days later. We kept the menu simple: macaroni and cheese and a side salad. We did this for two reasons. One, because we're kids and not professional chefs. And two, because we didn't want the cooking to get in the way of our real objectives.

Lauren and I worked on getting the meal ready while Grandma sat at the kitchen table filling out a crossword puzzle. I kept my eyes glued to the oven clock while I stirred the pot of boiling noodles.

As soon as it hit 6:59, I knew that, based on Connor's recon, my grandpa would be walking through the kitchen doorway any second, and Lauren and I would have to get to work on something other than dinner.

I went to signal Lauren but stopped when I noticed Grandma looking up from her crossword puzzle.

"First Connor and Josh keep us company for a whole week, and now you two are making us dinner," Grandma said. "We must be the luckiest grandparents in the world."

"You guys do so much for us," Lauren said. "It's the least we could do."

"Yeah," I agreed. "We're the lucky ones."

"You two are just so nice," Grandma said with a smile. "I remember when you were both little and couldn't get along for nothing."

Lauren and I shared a look: It was a lot more recent than our grandma remembered. It was a good thing she didn't remember, or she definitely would've been a lot more suspicious.

"You know what?" I said. "I actually forgot about that."

"Yeah, me too," Lauren agreed.

Grandma returned to her crossword puzzle. With her eyes on the paper, she said, "I never will. For a long time, I was really worried about you two. I thought you'd never get along."

"You don't gotta worry about us, Grandma," I said as I gestured to the oven clock to make sure Lauren was aware of the time.

Lauren nodded, her game face on. She was ready.

"I can't help but worry," Grandma said without looking up. "I'm your grandmother. It's my job."

"We appreciate it," Lauren said. "But we're good."

"Never better," I said, watching the clock as it struck 7:00.

Right on schedule, Grandpa sauntered into the kitchen on his way to the upstairs bathroom. "Those damn squirrels are at it again," he said. "I need to get my BB gun tomorrow and put a little lead in them. That'll teach them to stop eating from the bird feeder and setting off the motion detector."

In reality, it wasn't squirrels that were setting off his motion detectors—it was Ryan. Ryan had come along with Lauren and me and was using our visit as a distraction to double-check the motion detectors' range and his gap theory. I crossed my fingers that his setting the detectors off wasn't a sign that his theory had been incorrect.

"Be nice to the squirrels, Joseph," Grandma said.

"Don't worry," Grandpa said with a grin. "I will. I'll be real nice." He turned to Lauren and me. "Where do we stand on the grub? Need any squirrel meat?"

"Ew," Lauren said with a cringe.

"I think we'll be fine without it," I said. "And the noodles should be ready in a couple minutes."

"Good. So will I," Grandpa said and then started for the hallway.

"Don't forget to crack the window," Grandma said.

Grandpa shook his head. "A guy forgets to open a window once forty years ago."

"And you haven't forgotten since."

"I haven't had the chance. Let this be a lesson to you, Mitch."

"Sure, Grandpa," I said, although I wasn't exactly sure what the lesson actually was. In fact, I'm still not sure what it was.

Grandpa continued on his way. Once he was gone, I nodded to Lauren: It was time to get started.

"Well, I'm pretty much done with the salad," Lauren said. "I'm gonna check ESPN really quick. I think there was a big trade or score or something like that." She smiled at Grandma as she exited the room.

🎁 🎁 🎁

It's debatable what's more stressful, pulling a job or being the lookout. On one hand, there's a bigger risk of getting caught in the act, and the lookout can always maintain plausible deniability. But on the other hand, at least the person pulling the job knows what's going on.

Minutes had passed, and I had no clue what was happening, except that it was taking Lauren a lot longer than I'd expected. It was only supposed to take thirty seconds for the superglue to dry.

I couldn't help but stare at the clock. When it reached 7:05, I was sweating from more than the steam wafting out of the boiling, pasta-filled water.

"Make sure you don't overcook the noodles," Grandma said, her voice snapping me to attention.

"Oh, yeah," I said. "Good call."

I turned off the stove and dumped the water into the strainer. My focus immediately shifted back to the time. My mind raced, trying to figure out what was taking Lauren so long. Had something gone wrong? And if so, what? My heart was thumping two hundred beats per minute. I swore it was gonna burst like a water balloon.

Grandma looked up from her crossword. It must have been obvious I was struggling because she asked, "Are you all right?"

"Yeah," I said. I took a deep breath. "I just really want this dinner to be good."

"Don't worry, I'm sure it's going to be great," she said. "Maybe you can help me with this crossword. Do you know a five-letter word for 'a con's job'? The first two letters are S and C."

"No. I don't think so," I said, trying to play it cool. But inside, my stomach was twisting into knots. The answer was obviously "score." What were the odds that that answer would come up in a crossword puzzle while we were trying to pull one off? Slim to none, at best. I convinced myself that the fix was in and that she was just messing with me. This seemingly sweet old lady that I knew as Grandma had secretly been on to us. She knew that Lauren and I didn't get along, and she was about to blow the lid off of everything.

"Hmmm," Grandma said innocently . . . a little too innocently. "All I can think of is 'scams,' but that's plural. 'Scheme'? No. That's six letters. 'Scope'?"

"Score," I blurted out. If it was a setup, I just wanted it to be over. "It's probably score. But maybe not. I don't know."

"What do you know? That actually fits. Good job. How did you think of that?"

"I don't know. It just popped in my head."

"Well, I'm glad it did. Thank you," Grandma said and then quietly returned to her crossword puzzle.

I sighed. She wasn't actually on to us. I'd obviously just let my anxiety build so much that it morphed into full-blown paranoia. I wiped the sweat from my brow and quietly let out a deep exhale to calm myself even more, but the tiny sense of relief I got was short-lived.

Just a few seconds later, Grandpa strolled back into the kitchen. "What popped into your head?" he asked.

"Hey, Grandpa!" I shouted. My explosion was part being caught off-guard, and part warning shot to Lauren. She needed to know that Grandpa was already back, and that she really needed to hurry up!

Startled, Grandpa stumbled backwards and covered his ears with cupped hands. "What in the hell are you yelling for?" he said. "My hearing isn't that bad, you know."

"Sorry," I said. "I didn't expect you to be back so quick."

"Yeah, well, you can chalk that up to the magic of prune juice," he said. "It's like David Copperfield in a bottle."

Grandpa started for the living room. I knew I needed to stall him, but I didn't have a plan. So I just shouted, "Grandpa!"

His whole body jolted from the sound.

"Sorry for yelling again," I apologized. "But do you mind testing the pasta?"

Grandpa's eyes narrowed. He stared at me for a second. I'm not sure what he was thinking, probably that I was the biggest weirdo of all of his grandkids. Whatever he was thinking, I didn't care and would have been happy to let him stay trapped in his thoughts for as long as he needed. It was just buying me the time that I needed. And buying time is buying time, even if it costs you your grandpa's respect.

"Just taste the pasta already," Grandma insisted.

Grandpa shrugged. "Why not? You know, there's nothing worse than a limp noodle." He chuckled to himself. "You'll get that joke when you're older. Although, hopefully, you don't actually 'get' that joke. If you know what I mean."

"Yeah," I said, even though I didn't. It was just another one of his jokes that flew a couple feet over my head.

"Give me your best noodle."

I used a fork to pluck a piece of pasta from the strainer. "You need to wait a second, though. They're still really hot."

"I'm sure it's fine." He went to reach for the noodle.

"No, seriously," I said as I pulled the fork back. "Just let me blow on it for a little." I gave a slow and gentle blow.

Grandpa impatiently tapped his foot.

"Just a couple more," I said. "I don't want it to burn your mouth." I gave it five long blows. After each blow, I stealthily glanced beyond Grandpa, hoping to see Lauren hurrying back into the kitchen. Each time, my hopes were dashed. And while I successfully burned up a good fifteen seconds with my tactics, I also burned all of Grandpa's patience.

"This is taking too long," Grandpa said. He moved faster than I anticipated and yanked the noodle from the fork. He threw it into his mouth and chewed. "It's perfect. You're a regular Mario Batali." He patted me on the back and headed for the living room.

"Maybe you should try another. Just to make sure," I said with an overly eager smile.

"Let your grandma," he said. "I don't want to spoil my dinner."

"Uh," I said, trying to come up with another excuse, but I was out of ideas and Grandpa was almost out the door. My body tensed as the panic set in.

❄ CHAPTER THIRTEEN ❄

WHILE NEITHER OF my grandparents is as skilled at interrogations as my mom, they aren't complete pushovers either. As soon as Grandpa disappeared through the kitchen threshold, I immediately began working on my defense. Like usual, I mostly just spun my wheels without much progress.

Thankfully, this time, I didn't need it.

Less than half a second after Grandpa left, there was a loud thud. Grandpa stumbled back into the room, followed by a hard-charging Lauren. "I'm so sorry," she said as she tried to help support Grandpa.

"What in God's name are you running from?" Grandpa said.

"Uh, Skip Bayless and Stephen A. Smith were on TV," Lauren said. "I couldn't take it. I had to get out of there."

Grandpa's face dropped. "What? Seriously?"

Lauren nodded rapidly.

"Did you change the channel?" Grandpa said, a strange and unfamiliar fear in his voice.

"No," Lauren said. "I didn't have a chance."

"You have to change the channel! I have a Nielsen box. That will show up in the ratings." Grandpa scurried out of the kitchen.

Lauren and I shared a look: That was way too close. I mouthed, "What happened?"

She mouthed back, "I'll tell you later."

Whatever had happened, it was in the past, and in the present, I had something that I needed to do.

"Everything is basically ready," I said. I took off my apron and handed it to Lauren. "All you need to do is add the cheese and milk."

"Where are you going?" Grandma asked as I started toward the hallway.

I stopped. "I was gonna go to the bathroom upstairs."

"Enter at your own risk," Grandma said as she shook her head. "And make sure the window is still cracked."

"I will," I said, and then continued out of the kitchen and down the hall to the stairway. My foot had barely hit the first step when I realized what Grandma was talking about and why she was so adamant about the window. I was smacked with a thick wall of odor.

I know that hot air rises and cold air falls, but somehow smelly air seems to travel in every direction. Someone, preferably a professional scientist, should really look into that. It seems like it totally defies all the laws of physics. At least the little that I know about them.

As much as I wanted to wait it out, there wasn't any time to waste. I clamped my nostrils shut with my fingers and then bounded up the stairs.

The first place I checked was my grandparents' room. I figured the logic that all parents hide things in their rooms would hold with grandparents. After all, they had been parents—and were still parents, technically.

I searched the closet. All I found were tons of old clothes. I dug through every hiding space in the rest of the room. There was no sign of the presents.

It dawned on me that I wasn't dealing with just one or two kids' presents. There were seven of us. They wouldn't be able to use their old hiding spots.

The presents would take up too much space, like a whole room. In that case, they would have to be in one of the guest rooms.

I checked out the first guest room. It was empty. I mean, there was stuff, just not any presents.

The second guest room was more of the same. I was getting worried. There was only one room left.

I darted to the third guest room. It was no different from the others. No presents.

I knew that they couldn't have put the presents in the basement. It was too damp down there, and they could get ruined. If they were at my grandparents', they had to be upstairs. The only other possibility was—they weren't there. I started to hyperventilate. Had I misheard my parents? Or, even worse, had I been wrong about the pickup date? Had it already come? Was my PlayStation 4 gone for good? All those thoughts cycled through my head in rapid succession.

I retrieved Lauren's cell phone from my pocket. She'd lent it to me just in case I needed any outside assistance, which was exactly what I needed. My fingers nervously fumbled to pull up Ryan's contact info. After a couple accidental screen taps, I was finally able to click Ryan's profile and hit call.

"Great news," Ryan said as he answered his phone, not even giving me a chance to speak. "I was right about the gaps. We got a clean shot."

"That's great," I said. "But unfortunately, I think I was wrong about the presents."

"What do you mean?" Ryan demanded, his upbeat mood turning sour on a dime.

"The presents aren't here," I said.

"But you told us they were gonna be there."

"I know what I said. And now I'm telling you what I see. I've searched all the bedrooms. They aren't here."

"You checked the closets?"

"Of course."

"And under the beds?"

"Yes. I checked everything."

"So you checked the attic?"

I froze for a second. I hadn't checked the attic. But only because I didn't even know there was one. "What attic?" I asked.

"The one above Grandma and Grandpa's bedroom," Ryan said.

"Give me a second," I said. I darted into my grandparents' room. The cord to the retractable attic stairs dangled from above. "I guess I forgot to check the attic."

"Well, check it!"

"Okay! I'm going to. I gotta go."

I hung up the phone and slid it back into my pocket. I reached for the cord to the retractable stairway and gave it a gentle tug. The stairs unfolded with a soft metallic whine. I caught them and gently set them on the carpet. I stared up at the pitch-black hole in the ceiling that the stairs led to.

I'm pretty sure I already told you I don't like the dark, right? I mean, I can be in the dark with other people, just not by myself. Unfortunately, I was by myself. I had to go alone.

I took a deep breath and climbed the unstable stairs, doing my best to make as little noise as possible. Once I reached the attic, I swiped my hand in the darkness until I found the string for the light and turned it on.

At first, all I saw were a bunch of cardboard boxes—most likely old family pictures, report cards, and things like that—but as I turned my head, I finally found what I'd been looking for. In the corner of the attic, stacked like a fortune in gold bullion, was our pile of presents.

"Jackpot," I said to myself as I took in the awesomeness of the stash of gifts.

🎁 🎁 🎁

I did my best to keep a low profile for the rest of dinner. But it was hard, I was practically bubbling over with unexpressed excitement. I knew that we still had a lot of work to do before the PlayStation was in my possession, but I couldn't help getting swept up in it all. Everything was falling into place. And just because they say not to count your chickens before they hatch doesn't mean you can't think about the chickens, right? I mean, that's not the same thing as counting.

After we'd finished dinner, Lauren and I helped with the dishes, and then we all said our goodbyes.

"Drive safe," Grandpa said, laughing at his own joke as Lauren and I exited the house.

"Don't worry, we will," I said with a forced chuckle.

We started down the path to the driveway. I still hadn't had a chance to tell Lauren the great news. And even though she had to have assumed that I'd found the presents by the way that I'd acted, I could tell she was just as eager to get a verbal confirmation, as I was to hear what had happened with the magnet.

Lauren started to say something, but I quickly and quietly shushed her. I had a feeling our grandparents would be watching us from the door for a while.

Old people love to do that. I glanced over my shoulder to see if the coast was clear.

It's a good thing that I'd shushed Lauren because the coast was anything but clear. Our grandparents were still waiting in the doorway. They both waved. I smiled and waved back. They gave me one last little wave before finally heading inside.

I stopped as soon as I heard the door shut. "What happened?" I asked.

"I was just about to ask you the same thing," Lauren said.

Before either of us could say another word, Ryan popped out of the bushes.

Startled, Lauren and I jumped back. Although, I think I actually jumped more up than back. In fact, I don't think I've ever jumped that high in my life, or probably ever will. I honestly think I could have dunked on a real ten-foot basketball hoop. Okay, I might be exaggerating a little. But still, it was pretty high.

"Are you kidding me, Ryan?" Lauren snapped. She slapped him in the arm. "You can't sneak up on people like that in the dark."

"Seriously," I agreed as I tried to reclaim my breath.

"Sorry," Ryan said. "So what happened?"

Lauren looked to me for an answer.

"I asked you first," I said.

"Fine," she said. "I almost got caught by Grandpa because of this stupid glue." Lauren pulled the tube of Krazy Glue from her pocket and held it up for Ryan and me to see.

I squinted, trying to read it without any luck. "It's too dark," I said.

"Yeah," Ryan agreed. "And the writing looks really small."

"Well, if you could read it," Lauren said, "you'd see that it says that you need to hold what you're gluing in place for thirty seconds, but then you gotta let it dry for five minutes."

"Oh," I said. "My bad. I didn't see that."

"It's okay. All's well that ends well. Assuming both of your missions ended well too."

"Mine did," Ryan said.

"Good."

"And mine ended more than well," I said. I retrieved Lauren's cell from my pocket and handed it to her so they could see the picture I'd taken of the pile of presents. "They're all up there."

"Wow," Lauren said.

"It's the most beautiful thing I've ever seen," Ryan said.

"Yeah," I agreed. "And it's all within reach."

❆ CHAPTER FOURTEEN ❆

ALL OF THE cousins spent the next few days helping with the decoys, and then, on the eve of Christmas Eve, Ryan, Lauren, and I swung by Floyd's house to pick up the bike strollers. We met Floyd in his garage just after his parents had left for a holiday party.

The garage was actually more of a workshop than a garage. There must have been fifty bikes, all of them in various stages of assembly, and all of them much nicer than the ones that we'd ridden over on.

"You're all set," Floyd said as he gave his wrench one more tug and finished attaching the last stroller to my bike. "You got the list?"

"Yeah," I said, and then handed him the list of all of our presents.

Floyd smiled to himself as he skimmed over the sheet of paper. "Well, well, well," he said. "You guys sure have some good taste."

"Only the underlined stuff is yours," Lauren reminded him.

"Don't worry. I figured that much," Floyd said. "I'd say we're all making out pretty nicely. You guys should try to lose your presents every year." He flashed a cocky grin.

We all shot Floyd unappreciative looks. Lauren held up a clenched fist for added effect.

Floyd's smirk disappeared in less than a millisecond. "I'll, uh, leave the garage door unlocked," he said. "You can drop off my cut anytime."

🎁　🎁　🎁

Lauren, Ryan, and I hauled our butts back to Claire's house. When we got to Claire's room, the other cousins were huddled around Connor, who was putting the finishing touches on a decoy.

"What's our status?" I asked.

"TBD," Noah said as he and Claire inspected the present together.

"The shape is perf," Claire said.

"Totes," Noah agreed. It was one of the many terms that he'd picked up in his time with Claire, along with a couple "products" that he was using in his hair. I'm not saying he was better for it, just that they'd clearly rubbed off on each other. He hefted the present. "So is the weight. Would you like to do the honors, Claire?"

"Only if you insist."

"I do."

Noah handed Claire the package. She gave it a little jiggle, considered it for a second, and then gave it a much firmer jiggle. Claire smiled and said, "That will definitely pass for The Amazing Spider-Man motorized web-shooting Spider-Man."

"Not bad for an old day planner, four boxes of raisins, and a roll of pennies," Connor said with a grin of his own.

Noah made a check mark on his list. "That does it," he said. "That's all the presents."

We all celebrated like we'd just won the Super Bowl, or at the very least, a really good game of flag football. There were high-fives and group hugs all around.

After the celebration winded down, I steered the ship back to the next task at hand. "Now that we're done," I said, "we just need to move the presents to the tree house."

"I have a little something to help with that," Claire said, unable to hide her excitement. She went to her closet and pulled out seven oversize Christmas stockings.

Each stocking had a different cousin's name sewn on it and was big enough to fit all of their toys. I'd never admit this to my mom, but they looked even better than the stockings that she'd made for Connor and me when we were toddlers.

"Where'd you get those?" I asked.

"I made them last night," Claire said.

"They're awesome," Lauren said.

"Yeah," Ryan agreed. "I don't know if they'd be popular in L.A., but I think they're super cool." He patted Claire on the shoulder.

Claire's cheeks blushed a little. "Thanks," she said.

"All right, guys," I said. "No time to waste. Let's stuff these stockings and get them on the road."

We did just that, filling the stockings with each cousin's respective gifts and then loading them into the bike strollers.

🎁 🎁 🎁

When we finally made it to my house, my parents were in the living room listening to Christmas music. We could have tried to sneak past them on our own, but we decided it was better to play it safe.

"Connor, you're gonna need to distract them," I said.

"With what?" he said.

"I don't know." And then an idea popped in my head. "I got it! Ask them about the elf on the shelf. You noticed they put it out last week, right?"

"Yeah."

"Well, why? I mean, why would the elf need to report to Santa if Santa already knows we aren't getting gifts?"

"That's a great point!" Connor exclaimed. He took off for the house and scurried inside.

From the street, I watched as Connor pointed to the plush elf that sat on the mantel. My parents squirmed as they tried to get each other to answer the question. I could have watched it for hours, but Lauren gave me a nudge, reminding me that there was still work to do.

"Right," I said. "Let's do this."

Lauren, Ryan, and I pedaled our presents to the backyard. Noah, Josh, and Claire sprinted behind us.

🎁 🎁 🎁

Connor rejoined the crew just as we finished loading the last stocking into the tree house. "That worked like a charm," he said with a grin.

"Yeah, it did. Good job," I said. I turned to face the rest of the group. "All right, guys. Now that we've got everything ready, we just need to execute.

The pageant starts at six tomorrow. Grandma and Grandpa should be out of their house by 5:40. I want us in by 5:41. That means everyone needs to meet here by 5:20 sharp, and we leave no later than 5:25. Anyone not here by then gets left behind. Got it?"

Everyone nodded.

"Make sure to get a lot of sleep tonight," Lauren added. "You might even want to consider carbo-loading so you don't have an energy crash. Also, stay hydrated and have a banana or two."

"Good call," I said. "And remember, if we all stick to the schedule and do our jobs, this time tomorrow night we'll be opening presents."

The thought of opening presents got the younger cousins fired up. "Presents!" Connor cheered as he pumped his fist. "Presents! Presents!"

Noah and Claire joined in the cheer while Josh pumped his fist in rhythm to their chants.

Ryan smirked, soaking up the younger cousins' enthusiasm. He turned to Lauren and me. "In some ways, I envy kids," he said. "They're so happy. So free of all the stresses of the real world. They don't realize how good they have it."

"You realize you're still a kid, right?" Lauren said. She quickly covered when she saw the smile on Ryan's face start to fade. "But you're basically an adult too. Much more of an adult than we are."

Ryan's smile returned. "That is true."

I leaned in toward Ryan's chin and squinted. "I actually think I see a second hair poking through."

"Don't mess with me," Ryan said, super serious.

"I'm not. Your hair is getting a friend."

Lauren examined Ryan's chin for herself. "Unless I'm looking at the same hair, there might even be a third."

"You might be right," I said.

"Are we all good here?" Ryan excitedly asked.

"Yeah. We're good."

"Cool. 'Cause I gotta go check this out. I'll see you tomorrow, Mitch." With that, Ryan bolted from the tree house.

I turned to Lauren and smiled. "I really saw a hair."

"Sure, you did," Lauren said with a grin. "I have something for you." She dug in her pocket and pulled out one of the gold medals that I'd seen hanging on her trophy wall.

"What is that?" I said.

"It's the Floor General Award I won at an AAU tournament last summer," Lauren said. "I got it after setting a record for the most assists."

"You don't have to give it to me."

"I'm not giving it to you. You've been such a great Floor General, you've earned it." She handed me the medal.

"Wow. Thanks," I said as I took in the medal. It was the first award I'd ever received. It felt good. No, it felt better than good. It felt great.

"I really underestimated you," Lauren said. "We wouldn't be where we are without your ideas and leadership."

"Yeah, well, if I had a medal for anything, not counting the medal you just gave me, I'd give it to you for being the best teammate. 'Cause there's no way I could have done all this alone."

We shared a smile. It was really something. After a lifetime of butting heads, we were finally getting along. And not just for show, we genuinely appreciated each other. It was a pretty amazing turnaround.

"So does this mean we're gonna stop pretending that we aren't cousins when we're at school?" I asked.

"I actually already told a bunch of people that we were," Lauren said.

"Really?" I said, surprised.

"Yeah. My friends kept asking me why I wasn't hanging out with them. So I kinda had to tell them."

"Oh," I said, my smile fading. "That makes sense."

Lauren must have noticed that I was a little upset because she quickly added, "But I would've told them anyway, cousin." She grinned at the end, emphasizing the "cousin" part.

The smile returned to my face. "Me too, cousin."

"All right," Lauren said. "Well, we should all probably head home. Tomorrow's gonna be a long day."

"Yeah," I agreed.

All of the remaining cousins followed Lauren out of the tree house. Connor and I made it back inside our house just in time for dinner. We both plowed through the meal and then went straight to bed. I had no desire to fight my curfew like usual. I wanted to get sleeping out of the way. The sooner I went to bed, the sooner I'd wake up, and the sooner I'd get my PlayStation back.

Of course, it always works out that when you don't want to fall asleep, you always do. And when you actually want to fall asleep, you usually end up staring at the ceiling for hours on end. That's what I did for a good hour or two while visions of PlayStations and video games danced in my head.

Eventually, the soft rustling of the trees in the front yard swaying in the breeze put me to sleep.

The next morning, I woke up with a smile and hopped out of bed with an extra spring it my step. It was gonna be great day, I could feel it. I was in the middle of doing my morning yawning and stretching when I noticed something completely unexpected.

The window to my room was frosted over. Except it wasn't just frost—there was snow!

I rushed to the window. Sure enough, the whole neighborhood was blanketed in by least a foot of fresh white powder. I gazed in amazement, not fully realizing the significance. And then it all hit me like a snowball, or even worse, like an ice ball, or one hundred ice balls that had been chucked at the same time.

WE GOT A FOOT OF SNOW!

I'm sure there are kids reading this in Minnesota or Wisconsin who are probably thinking, "A foot of snow? Big deal." And that might be true for Minnesota and Wisconsin. But that isn't the case for Northern Virginia. Our schools pretty much shut down when someone even mentions the possibility of snow. The person doesn't even have to be credible, not that most meteorologists are. But I wasn't worried about school, which was already closed for the holidays. I was worried about the heist.

There was no way that we would be able to ride our bikes in that much snow. Which meant that the bike strollers were useless. Which meant that we had no way to transport all of the presents. Which also meant that I had no idea what we were gonna do.

⚜ CHAPTER FIFTEEN ⚜

AFTER FIVE SOLID minutes of panic, which is probably pretty reasonable for any kid in that position, I sprinted downstairs to the kitchen. I was just about to grab the phone when it rang.

I checked the caller ID. It was Lauren.

I answered the phone. "I was just about to call you."

"Is the line secure?" Lauren said.

"Hold on a second."

Most parents have a strong need to answer the phone even if it stops ringing. My parents were no different. Like clockwork, my mom hopped on the line exactly five seconds after the last ring.

"Who is it?" my mom asked.

"It's Lauren," I said. "I got it."

"Hi, Lauren."

"Hi, Aunt Karen," Lauren replied.

"Can you tell your mother to call me later?"

"Of course."

"Thank you."

A couple seconds of silence passed, and then I asked, as politely as I could, "Is that it, Mom?"

"Yes," my mom said. "Okay. Bye, Lauren."

"Bye, Aunt Karen," Lauren replied.

Not realizing that parents are also prone to hanging on the line and eavesdropping, an inexperienced kid would have started talking right away. But Lauren and I were smarter than that. We made sure to wait until we heard the click, and then we waited a couple more seconds just to be extra safe.

"I think we're good," I said.

"No, we aren't," Lauren said.

"I meant about the phone."

"Well, now I'm talking about the snow. Of all the years to have a white Christmas!"

"I know. There hasn't been snow for Christmas in like six years."

"How did we not see this coming?"

"'Cause we're kids," I said. "We don't pay attention to the weather. That's what old people do."

It's true. I don't know if you've ever noticed how much old people obsess over the weather, but they do. My parents are always making me put on The Weather Channel when I'm trying to watch TV. At that moment, I wished I were an old person, or that Ryan had acted as old as he claimed to be.

"What are we gonna do?" Lauren said. "We can't ride our bikes in this. The trailers are useless."

"I know. Let me think about it." I thought about it for a couple seconds. It took me longer than it should have to come up with the solution you probably already reached, but only because it's a lot harder to think when you're under a ton of pressure. "Duh," I said, finally realizing the answer. "We need sleds. Do you guys have any?"

"No. We gave ours away last year."

"I have one. It's a decent size, but we're gonna need at least one more. I'll check with Noah and Claire. You call everyone you know."

I called Noah, but he didn't have a sled. Apparently, his mom decided that they were too dangerous. Noah also agreed and said that the statistics supported her belief.

While I didn't agree with Noah or his mom, I didn't have time to debate him. I just hung up and called Claire, who said she had one sled, but that it was a Barbie sled from when she was three. She said that at most it could carry one present.

That didn't help us at all.

I called Lauren back on her cell phone. "Any luck with your friends?"

"No," she said. "I'm assuming the same for Noah and Claire."

"Yeah."

"What about your friends?"

"I really only have one good friend, and I already know he doesn't have a sled." As soon as the words left my mouth, I realized someone who did. "The Shark! He has a sled. It's a huge one too. I saw it behind some of the bikes in his garage."

"First off, don't humor him and call him that," Lauren said. "He's Floyd. Little, annoying Floyd. And second, there's gotta be someone else we can go to who we just haven't thought of yet."

"Yeah, and we might never think of them. We don't have time."

"I'd rather not deal with that kid again. He rubs me the wrong way."

"He rubs everyone the wrong way," I said. "It's the only way he rubs people. But he's probably our only option."

Lauren took a moment before finally agreeing. "Fine," she groaned. "I'll meet you at his house in fifteen minutes."

"Cool. I'll give him a ring and make sure he's there."

🎁　🎁　🎁

Floyd opened his front door before we could even knock. "Come right in," he said with an eager grin. It was clear that he'd been waiting for our arrival since the moment I'd called to ask him about the sled.

Floyd led us to the garage and retrieved the sixty-inch Flexible Flyer sled that I'd spotted earlier. "Yep. She's a good one," he said. "She'll definitely help you guys out tonight."

"Perfect. We really appreciate you giving it to us, Shark," I said, throwing out his nickname to butter him up. But of course, the butter just melted.

"Pump the brakes, big guy," Floyd said. "I never said I was 'giving' it to you. Quite the opposite. This is gonna cost you twice the original fee."

They say a fool is someone who does the same thing over and over and expects a different result. I guess that made me a fool, because I kept dealing with Floyd and kept expecting him not to be a complete jerk.

"You can't be serious," I said.

"Supply and demand," Floyd said. "You're free to shop elsewhere, but good luck finding a sled this nice on such short notice."

I saw Lauren's face turning beet red. While I'd gotten her to promise to let me do the talking, I knew that I couldn't expect her to keep up her end with Floyd being so Floyd-like. I was right.

"We shouldn't have to pay you at all," Lauren snarled. "The trailers are useless."

"And how's that my fault?" Floyd said. "I don't control the weather. A deal's a deal. Besides, we all know from school that there's no such thing as a free lunch."

"What if the lunch is a knuckle sandwich?" Lauren said. She balled up her fist and held it cocked.

Floyd's eyes bugged out of his head. "You could hurt your hand. That's a cost."

"I could," Lauren said, "but that doesn't mean I will for sure. And even if I did, maybe I'm fine paying that price."

Floyd swallowed hard. I quikcly shuffled between him and Lauren, breaking them up. I knew force wasn't gonna get us anywhere. "No one is getting knuckle sandwiches," I said. "And he's right, Lauren, about the free lunch and the deal."

Lauren gave me the same look that she'd given Floyd. It had been a while since I'd seen her anger directed at me. I'd even forgotten how intimidating it was.

"I mean, he's right, to an extent," I corrected myself. "But he's forgetting the fact that we're in this together. We're partners. That's right, Floyd. If we don't get our presents, you don't get our unwanted presents. And then we all lose."

"Hmmm," Floyd said, "So what you're saying is that I'm incentivized to help you succeed."

"Yes, you are."

Floyd stared at us for a couple seconds while he considered his options. "It is quite the catch-22," he said. "All right. I'll drop my asking price."

"Thank you," I said.

"But!" Floyd held up his index finger. "And it's a big but." He chuckled at the double meaning of his words. "I get to pick one more present as payment."

"What do you want?" I asked, nervous that he might choose the PlayStation. It was by far the most valuable item on list. It was the obvious choice. I held my breath in anticipation.

Floyd pulled our gift list from his pocket. "Well," he said as his skimmed over his options. "I'm a reasonable kid, so I won't ask for the PlayStation."

I quietly let out a sigh of relief.

Floyd continued, "But I do see there's a Kevin Durant jersey on here, and he is my favorite player."

Without seeing her reaction, I was pretty sure it was Lauren's gift. Seeing her reaction only confirmed my belief.

"Are you insane?" Lauren said. "It won't even fit you."

"Don't worry about me," Floyd said. "I'll grow into it."

"That's assuming you live long enough." Lauren clenched her fists at her side.

I could see the veins in Floyd's neck bulge, but he held firm. "Arguably, none of us are guaranteed tomorrow—or anything, for that matter." He held up the list, as if to say that the presents weren't guaranteed.

"What if I say no?" Lauren asked through gritted teeth.

"Then there's a chance that I say no. But there's only one way to find out. Are you willing to risk going nuclear? Are you willing to push the button?"

"Hold on a second," I interrupted before Lauren could answer. I pulled her aside and out of Floyd's earshot. "I know you really WANT that jersey," I said, "but we NEED the sled."

"It's not just the jersey," Lauren sighed, frustrated. "I hate losing. Especially to jerks like him."

"Don't worry about that," I said. "The only way people like him ever win is when people like you let them. He's a mean kid. Trust me, his life is gonna be one disappointment after the next. This is as good as it gets for him."

Lauren glared at Floyd. She knew I was right.

All eyes on him, Floyd became super self-conscious. "Hey," he shouted. "What are you two talking about? Do we got a deal or not?"

Lauren thought about it for one more second. "Yeah," she said. "We have a deal."

"Great. Let's shake on it," Floyd said.

As they shook hands, a smirk crept across Floyd's face. He went to tighten his grip on Lauren's hand like he'd done to mine. It was a big mistake. Floyd not only underestimated Lauren's strength but also her pent-up aggression.

Lauren wasn't as kind as I'd been. She returned the favor tenfold, crushing Floyd's hand so hard that he dropped to his knees, which only encouraged her to tighten her grip even more.

"What's with you guys?" Floyd whined. "I was just trying to shake your hand."

Lauren gave one final squeeze, her strongest, and then let go. She stormed out of the garage. I grabbed the sled and chased after her.

I caught up to Lauren just before the end of the driveway. "Thanks," I said.

"You don't need to thank me," she said. "We're all in this together. You would have done the same thing."

Would I? I wasn't as confident as Lauren. I mean, if Floyd had demanded a jersey I wanted? Yeah, I could have given that up. But if he would have gone for my PlayStation? There's no way I would've agreed to that. We'd have been down a sled for sure. Of course, I didn't tell Lauren that. Instead, I just agreed.

"Yeah. Of course," I said. "Anyway, it's still gonna be tough with just two sleds. We really need to make sure we stay on schedule."

"I'll call everyone and tell them to be at your place by 5:00 instead of 5:20."

"Good thinking."

"And Ryan and I will be there at 4:50 to help you load everything up."

"Awesome. I'll see you then."

Lauren and I bumped gloved fists and then headed on our separate ways.

🎁 🎁 🎁

The hours dragged leading up to the heist. It felt like my parents were watching my every move. And there are few things harder than convincing your

173

parents that you aren't up to something when you clearly are up to something. In fact, I'd be willing to bet that most great actors got their starts by lying to their parents. The best acting job ever was probably Leonardo DiCaprio lying to his mom about a missing cookie or a broken window. My performance that day wasn't exactly Oscar-worthy, but it was good enough to get the job done, and that's all I needed.

While my parents finished getting ready to go to the pageant, I pulled Connor aside in the living room to give him the one last pep talk. "You're gonna do great," I said. "We couldn't do this without you. Here, take this." I slipped him a cell phone.

Connor inspected the phone's bedazzled, cheetah-print case and shot me a skeptical look. "Nice phone."

"It's obviously not mine." I shook my head. "It's Claire's. I can't believe you thought is was mine. Just make sure to call Lauren as soon as the pageant is over. Her number is the last one dialed."

"Okay."

"Hurry up, Pat," I heard my mom shout as she started down the stairs.

I gestured to Connor to stash the phone. He quickly slipped it into the pocket of his sheep costume just before our mom joined us. Getting caught with the phone wouldn't have been the end of us, but it definitely would have led to questions, and questions require answers. Even though we'd pulled it off, I knew we looked super shady.

"Hey," I said, trying to play it cool and deflate any suspicion.

My mom gave me a quick once-over and then shook her head. "I'm disappointed you aren't coming with us," she said. "But at least you're spending time with your cousins."

That was what we'd told our parents. After struggling to come up with the perfect story to free everyone up for the heist, Noah suggested just telling the truth, at least partially. He'd astutely observed that his parents never said no whenever he asked about going to Claire's. Not only that, they didn't even bother to ask him any details either. The rest of us realized that our parents had been just as easygoing with all things cousin related. And thankfully, they were equally easygoing when we told them that we were gonna hang out at my house for a little on Christmas Eve. Of course, my mom, while agreeable, wasn't exactly happy about it.

"Yep," I said to my mom with a casual nod, "just some quality time with the cousins." I readied my final poker face, which I'd practiced a few times just for that very moment.

Except my mom didn't even try to get a read on me. She just sighed, "Yeah," and then turned to the stairs. "We'll be waiting in the car," she yelled up to my dad, and the she and Connor headed for the front door.

I gave Connor a "hand phone" signal reminder and mouthed, "Call Lauren."

Connor nodded, flipped the hood on his sheep costume over his head, and the exited the house with my mom.

Seconds later, my dad flew down the stairs and out the door. I watched through the blinds as our SUV backed out of the driveway and drove off toward the setting sun.

With my parents gone, the clock had officially begun ticking. I changed into my darkest clothes, which I'd picked out before the snowstorm, a mistake in hindsight because they definitely weren't my warmest. I was reminded of that fact as I trudged through the snow to my tree house and climbed inside.

I plugged in the space heater to help warm things up and then checked my watch to get a sense of the time. It was 4:45. Lauren and Ryan would be arriving shortly, but I still had a couple minutes to myself.

I retrieved the decoy PlayStation from my stocking and hefted it. It really was a perfect match. If I didn't know it was a fake, I never would have guessed. I smiled to myself, proud of all the work we'd accomplished.

I returned the present to the stocking, took a seat on one of the tree house stools, and waited for my cousins to arrive. I kept my eyes peeled through the tree house window, searching the darkness for any signs of movement.

I waited a little and then checked my watch again. It was already 4:55. Lauren and Ryan were late. It wasn't how I'd wanted things to get started.

I'd heard the saying that a watched pot never boils, so I figured that maybe a watched cousin didn't arrive either. I got up from my stool and started to pace around the tree house. It was the only thing I could do to keep my mind from wandering and worrying.

I counted my laps, one lap for each time back and forth. When I got to one hundred, I checked my watch again. It was now 5:05, which meant that everyone was officially late. "So much for things going off without a hitch," I grumbled to myself.

So far, there had only been hitches.

I paced some more. Another hundred laps, another ten minutes passed, and not a single cousin arrived.

⚝ CHAPTER SIXTEEN ⚝

I KNEW THAT if I didn't stay busy, my mind would start to run wild. I reminded myself to just focus on what I could control. Just because the rest of the cousins hadn't arrived didn't mean that I couldn't get started without them.

One by one, I lowered the stockings from the tree house and loaded them onto the sleds. It was a lot harder than I'd expected it would be. Each of the stockings weighed somewhere between fifteen and thirty pounds. My arms got pretty tired, but I was able to get the job done.

I checked my watch when I finished. It was almost 5:25. There was still no sign of the others. I was starting to get really worried. I was also starting to get really angry.

With nothing to occupy myself with, I was no longer able to keep my mind from racing. What if something happened? What if one of the cousins get busted? What if the heist off?

Before I could go too far down the rabbit hole of what-ifs, Ryan and Lauren came sprinting along the side of the house.

"What the hell took you so long?" I snarled as they reached the backyard.

"I'm so sorry," Lauren said. "It was the snow. It really slowed us down."

"Yeah," Ryan said. "We ran the whole way over."

"Still, we should've left at least ten minutes ago. I thought you were gonna call everyone," I said to Lauren with more attitude than I probably intended. But what can I say? I was beyond frustrated.

"I said sorry," Lauren shot back. "And I did call everyone. Clearly the snow is slowing them down too. But since we obviously can't go back in time, we just need to make the best of our situation."

"Fine," I said, backing off a little. "Let's go now. We'll leave a note for the others and they can catch up. If they show."

"I don't think we're ready to go just yet," Ryan said as he stared at the overflowing sleds. "Those sleds look like the Grinch's sleigh after he swiped all the presents in Whoville. There's no way they'll stay on. We need to tie them down."

He had a good point. While the bike strollers had baskets to keep everything contained, the sleds had nothing to keep the stockings on. And if the stockings kept falling off while we were pulling the sleds, it would just slow us down even more.

"It's just one thing after another," I moaned. "I'll go find something. But we're leaving as soon as I get back."

I booked it to the back door of the house, kicked off my boots, and darted inside. I searched high and low, through every drawer and cabinet, but I couldn't find anything that was long enough to tie the presents down. As I closed the cabinet door above the microwave, I saw that it was just past 5:35. I wanted to scream. Nothing was going according to plan, and Ben Franklin was probably rolling over in his grave.

Thankfully, I caught the flicker of the lights on the Christmas tree, and it gave me an idea. I dug through my mom's bin of leftover decorations and pulled out as many strings of lights as I could. I quickly put the bin away and then bolted out the back door.

In my absence, Claire, Noah, and Josh had finally arrived.

"Nice of you guys to show up," I said as I rejoined the group.

"Take it easy," Lauren said. "Arguing is the last thing we need to do right now. We just need to get to Grandma and Grandpa's as fast as possible."

I was still livid about how everything was playing out, especially after the time it had taken me to come up with the lights, but Lauren was right. We didn't have time to argue. We barely had time for anything, including the heist.

"Start running," I ordered Claire, Noah, and Josh.

They all took off.

"You tie down that sled," I said as I tossed a string of lights to Ryan. "Lauren and I will get the other one."

Ryan went to work on securing his sled.

"You need to work on controlling your nerves," Lauren said as we fastened the stockings to our sled.

"I will."

"In high-pressure situations, your mental state can be the difference between winning and losing. Take a couple deep breaths."

I didn't listen; I just looked at her, still annoyed.

"Seriously," Lauren said. "Take a couple deep breaths."

I let some of my anger go. Who was I to question her? She'd been in way more high-pressure situations than I had. My only high-pressure situations were school tests, and I wasn't exactly a straight-A student. I took a couple deep breaths, and wouldn't you know, it actually helped. "Thanks," I said.

"No problem," Lauren said.

"I'm done," Ryan announced.

Seconds later, so were Lauren and I.

Ryan took off with his sled, and Lauren and I dragged ours. I checked my watch as we left my yard. It was 5:50. We were twenty-five minutes behind schedule, and we were only gonna fall even more behind on the trek to our grandparents. That was guaranteed. Another thing you could guarantee: There was no way we were gonna give up.

🎁 🎁 🎁

We trudged through the snow as fast as we could, which wasn't fast at all. Walking a mile in snow has to be equal to walking like ten miles on regular land, and both are equally terrible.

"My legs are burning," Noah whined.

"Pain is just weakness leaving the body," Lauren said.

"Then my body must be full of weakness," Claire moaned. "'Cause all I feel is pain."

"Come on, guys!" Lauren shouted. "Don't let a little snow stop you! We're almost there!"

I'm not sure if Lauren was just trying to motivate them or if she actually saw the towering holly tree, surrounded by a couple smaller evergreens, that was just a hundred yards ahead of us, but I'd spotted it a second earlier and recognized it almost immediately. It was our grandparents' tree.

I'd climbed the massive tree well over a hundred times. Grandpa always told us not to, but I would sneak into it anyway. It was prickly as hell and hurt to climb, but it was also the tallest tree around, so it was worth the discomfort.

"She's right," I said. I pointed toward the tree. "That's Grandma and Grandpa's holly tree."

"Yeah, it is," Ryan said.

"Yep. Just a little bit left," Lauren said to the struggling cousins. "You guys can do it. I know you can."

If there was any doubt before, it was now pretty apparent how Lauren had earned her Floor General award. She was a born leader, a captain, and she ran a tight ship.

"Ahhh!" Noah screamed as he fought through his exhaustion.

Claire joined in Noah's battle cry. While Josh didn't scream, you could see the sheer determination on his face.

When we finally made it to the wooded area, Claire, Noah, and Josh collapsed into a small snowbank.

"You can make all of the snow angels you want later," Lauren barked like a drill sergeant. "But this isn't playtime. It's go time!"

Claire, Noah, and Josh didn't hesitate. They picked themselves up off the ground as fast as they could.

Through the trees I could see the back door to our grandparents' house. "Lead the way, Ryan," I said.

"Follow me," Ryan said. He started to go but then stopped abruptly. "Oh, crap."

"What?" Lauren said.

"I just realized the pinecones I used to mark our path are definitely buried in the snow," Ryan said.

"How much clearance do we have on the other side of the trees?" I said.

"The motion sensors only reach fifty feet, so we got about twenty before we're in the danger zone. I made sure to put the cones right on the edge."

"All right. Then let's get through the trees, then we can dig for the cones."

Noah, Claire, and Josh cut through the trees first, followed by Ryan. As Lauren and I went to pull our sled through the wooded area, the sled seemed to fight back and didn't budge.

"Did you stop pulling?" Lauren asked.

"No. I think we're caught on a branch," I said.

"We need to give it a tug at the same time," Lauren said.

"Okay. I'll count down. One. Two. Three."

We yanked the sled at the same time. It broke free, and I went tumbling into the snow.

"What did I just say about snow angels?" Lauren said with a grin. "Save it for later."

"Very funny," I said, and then got back to my feet.

We pulled our sled and rejoined the others, who were already digging through the snow.

"I found one!" Claire said as she retrieved the first pinecone.

"Awesome," Ryan said. "The other one should be about four feet away on the right."

Ryan had barely finished when Josh hoisted the pinecone he'd found over his head.

"That's both of them," I said. "Let's go! Let's go!"

"Follow me," Ryan said.

We trailed Ryan as he cut a diagonal line right for the back door. We all made it to the door without tripping any of the motion detectors.

After Ryan used the key he'd swiped from his mom's keychain to unlock the deadbolt and doorknob, Lauren handed me a stethoscope.

"Your turn, Magneto," she said.

I took a deep breath, put the stethoscope on, and held the chest piece to the door with one hand. With my other hand, I rubbed a neodymium magnet over the door, listening carefully for the familiar click of the two tiny but powerful magnets attracting. I had easily matched the magnets while practicing on my bedroom door, but the thicker door at our grandparents' proved to be more difficult. Adding to the door issues was the fact that my heart was beating so fast that it caused my eardrums thump and hindered my hearing.

As I kept searching, I swore I heard a faint sound and decided to roll with it. I slid the lock into place just like I'd practiced, and then flipped the magnet to reverse the pole and, hopefully, spring the lock.

"Did it work?" Lauren asked, a little worry in her voice.

"I don't know," I said. "Time for the moment of truth."

I turned the handle and gave the door a gentle push. It opened right up. I let out a sigh of relief. Finally, something had gone right. The cousins congratulated me with pats on the back.

"No time to celebrate," I said. "We're still way behind schedule, and the pageant will be over in just about twenty minutes."

"He's right," Lauren said. "We need to haul butt for real."

We worked together to quickly untie the light strings and unload the sleds. Ryan rushed inside with three stockings slung over his shoulder. Noah struggled with one of the smaller stockings. Lauren gave him support while carrying a stocking of her own.

"Thanks," Noah said.

"Anytime," Lauren replied.

Josh, Claire, and I were left with the last stocking.

"I got the stocking," I said. "Josh, you watch the back door. Claire, you keep your eyes on the front." They both nodded in acknowledgment, and I hurried off with my stocking in tow.

By the time I made it to our grandparents' bedroom, Ryan had already lowered the attic stairs and was halfway up them, with Lauren just behind him.

"You hand me the stockings," Lauren said, "and I'll pass them to Ryan."

"Perfect," I said.

I gave Lauren my stocking, which she passed to Ryan.

I turned to Noah, expecting him to have the next stocking ready. But instead, his eyes were fixed on Lauren's boots.

"Noah!" I barked. "Get your head in the game."

"It is," Noah said. "And we have problem."

The last thing we needed was another problem. "What now?" I groaned.

Noah pointed to the pool of water forming on the ground under Lauren's boots. I noticed there was a similar collection of water around my boots too.

"We forgot to take off our shoes," Noah said. "We most likely tracked water all over the house."

He was right. We were so busy rushing that we got sloppy. It was just another thing we had to make up for. Another thing that was gonna slow us down and increase our chances of being busted. I had to bite my lip to keep myself from cursing.

"All right," I said, and then took a deep breath. "You, Claire, and Josh need to wipe up any water, and we'll handle the presents."

Noah nodded and then sped off.

I grabbed another stocking and handed it to Lauren. As I went to grab the next stocking, Lauren's phone started ringing. "I really hope that's just one of your friends," I said.

Lauren retrieved her phone and checked the caller ID. She shook her head. "It's Connor," she said, and then tossed me the phone.

I caught it and answered. "Please tell me you aren't done already."

"We aren't done already," Connor said.

"Really? Then why are you calling?"

"Because we're done already."

"Then why did you say you weren't?"

"Because you told me to."

I don't even want to get started, but six-year-olds can be so literal. I didn't want to get started with Connor either, so I just moved on. "Well, what's actually going on?" I asked.

"The pageant just finished," Connor said, "and everyone's starting to leave."

✦ CHAPTER SEVENTEEN ✦

I CHECKED MY watch. The pageant had ended fifteen minutes earlier than I'd expected. Of course it had. Why would it end when it was supposed to? Just about everything wasn't going according to plan. Why would the pageant be any different?

I struggled to run the numbers in my head: The number of minutes it would take for our grandparents to drive back home, minus the number of minutes we needed to finish the swap and get out. If you don't think kids nowadays are way too dependent on calculators, wait until you're in a stressful situation and then try to do simple subtraction. It's a hell of a lot harder than you think.

What made it even harder was that I kept getting a negative number. And I knew a negative number meant us getting caught red-handed. There was only one option.

"You gotta stall them," I said.

"Okay," Connor said.

But I could tell there was uncertainty in his voice.

"Do you know what that means?"

"I think so. You want me to get them in a bathroom stall?"

I had to hand it to him; it was a pretty creative answer. And it probably would've worked to "stall" our grandparents too, but it would have been close to impossible to pull off.

"No," I said. "That's not what it means at all. You just need to keep them busy."

"How?"

"Aren't they having refreshments or something afterwards?"

"I think so."

"Okay, well just make sure they go. And keep them there for as long as you can."

"Got it."

I hung up the phone and turned to Ryan and Lauren. "The pageant just finished," I said. "We need to put this gift swap into overdrive."

"We'll make it the fastest game of White Elephant ever," Lauren said confidently.

I summoned all of my strength and then some to grab two stockings and pass them to Lauren. She hoisted them up to Ryan. We used our little assembly line to get the rest of the stockings into the attic as fast as possible.

We ran a similar assembly line to switch out the presents. Ryan handed Lauren each decoy present, which she then gave to me. I swapped the decoy out for the real present, which I gave to her. She passed the real present back to Ryan, and then he stuffed the stocking.

One by one, we filled each of the stockings with the real gifts while moving at breakneck pace. The only time we slowed down even a little was when I swapped out my PlayStation. I couldn't help but soak it up for a split second.

Lauren got me back on track real quick. "Come on," she ordered. "You can stare it all you want later."

"I will," I said with a smile as I handed the real PlayStation to her. "Believe me, I will."

We were down to the last stocking when Lauren's phone rang again. "Is that Connor already?" Ryan asked.

I checked the caller ID. Thankfully, it wasn't Connor. "It says 'Cute Kevin.' Who's that?"

"Don't worry about it," Lauren said as she swiped her phone back and hit ignore.

"Wait. That's not Kevin Russell, is it?" I asked.

"No. It's probably Kevin McCallister," Ryan said. "He's a lot cuter. If we're being honest."

"I said don't worry about it," Lauren snarled. "Now can we stick to the task at hand?"

"Yeah, of course," I said.

But before we could get back to work, Lauren's phone rang again, and this time it wasn't "Cute Kevin." It was Connor.

Lauren answered the call. "What's up?" she said. She listened for a second. "And you can't do anything about it? Okay. Thanks." Lauren hung up and confirmed what Ryan and I already knew. "They're on their way home."

"That's okay," Ryan said. "We're almost done."

"Let's finish up and get out of here," I said.

And that was exactly what we did, swapping the gifts even faster than we had before. By the time we made our way down the retractable stairs with the newly filled stockings, Noah, Claire, and Josh were waiting in the bedroom with towels in hand.

"Noah, grab a stocking," I said. "Claire and Josh, you two make sure to wipe all of our tracks on the way out."

Claire and Josh scurried backwards on their hands and knees behind us as we all raced down the stairs, through the kitchen and family room, and then out the back door.

As we loaded the stockings on the sleds, I noticed that it had started to snow again, which was actually a good thing. "The flurries should slow down Grandma and Grandpa," I said.

"They should also help cover our tracks," Ryan added.

"Speaking of covering our tracks, I'll get the magnet."

"Good call," Lauren said. "Ryan and I will tie the stockings down."

She and Ryan fastened the stockings with the lights while I worked to pry the magnet from the chain lock with the flat-head screwdriver on my pocketknife.

"We got it all," Claire said as she and Josh finished up their mopping job. "What should we do with the towels?"

"Ditch them in the laundry room," I said.

Josh and Claire stuffed the towels in the heap of dirty clothes and bolted out the door just as I popped the magnet free. I pocketed the evidence and then shut the door.

"We're all here, right?" I said.

Noah did a hyperspeed head count. "Everyone is accounted for."

"Key me, Ryan," I said. He tossed me the key. I locked the knob and the deadbolt, and then tossed the key back. "All right, let's bounce."

But before we could even turn to leave, car headlights illuminated our exit path—our grand-parents were home.

Everyone's eyes went wide. I held my finger to my mouth, reminding them to stay quiet. After a couple seconds, the lights shut off, and then the doors to Grandpa's Buick open and shut.

"Trust me," I heard Grandpa say, "no one around here knows how to drive in the snow."

After a few more seconds, Grandpa's voice disappeared as he and Grandma entered the house and then closed the door.

"Hurry!" I whispered.

"Follow my footsteps," Ryan said as he pulled his sled and led the charge.

Lauren and I rushed with our sled behind him, followed closely by Josh and Noah. Claire brought up the rear.

We all collapsed to the ground in a heap as soon as we crossed into the safety zone.

"We made it," I said, gasping for air.

At least I'd thought we had. And then I saw Lauren's eyes dart through the pile of cousins. It was just a little bit smaller than it should have been. We had the same exact realization at the same exact time, but Lauren said it first. "Where's Claire?"

"Over here," Claire whispered.

We all turned our heads at once to find Claire balancing on one foot, her other shoeless foot held in the air. She was still a good ten feet from safety.

"What are you doing?" Ryan said.

"Yoga," Claire said sarcastically. "My boot got stuck."

Her green Hunter boot was submerged in the snow.

"Why didn't you wear boots with laces?" I said.

"Because they aren't as cute."

"They really aren't," Noah agreed.

I just shook my head.

"Don't worry, you can do this," Lauren said. "Just carefully slide your foot back into your boot." Claire followed Lauren's directions, but just like everything else that night, what seemed so simple proved to be much more difficult.

Claire's foot must have gotten caught in the heel part of her shoe because she lost her balance and tumbled into the snow, tripping the motion sensor in the process.

The spotlights blasted Claire.

Supposedly, there's a natural human response called "fight, flight, or freeze." When we find ourselves in harm's way, some of us will fight, some will fly, or run, and some will freeze. Unfortunately for us, Claire picked the last option. She just stared into the glowing bulbs like a deer in headlights.

"Run!" I urged Claire. But she just stayed on all fours in the snow, too stunned to move.

Lauren sprinted to our fallen cousin, hoisted Claire and her boot, and then dove back into the darkness.

Not a second later, one of the lights in the family room flicked on, and Grandpa stepped inside to investigate. We stayed completely still while he stared out of the bay window and into the backyard, looking right at us.

Chalk it up to the snow, the dark, or old age, but he didn't spot us. He just shook his head and went back into the kitchen.

We all let out heavy sighs of relief.

"That was way too close," Noah said.

"Good thing close only counts in Horseshoes and hand grenades," Ryan said.

"You know what this means, guys?" I said as a smile crossed my face. "We did it!"

All of the shock and adrenaline of almost getting caught turned to excitement as they realized that I was right. We'd pulled off our Christmas present heist.

"Yeah, we did!" Lauren said.

"I knew we could do it!" Ryan said. He pulled all of the cousins in for a big group hug.

"Merry Christmas, everyone," Noah said.

"And Happy Hanukkah," Claire added as she gave Noah an extra squeeze.

"Thanks," Noah said with a grin and squeezed her back.

I broke free from the hug. "All right, guys," I said. "Enough freezing our butts off. Let's get back to the tree house so we can really celebrate."

"Great idea," Lauren said.

We started for the wooded area at the corner of the yard. As we got close, Ryan noticed something and stopped. "What is that?" he said, pointing to a dark shadow hanging in the holly tree.

"I can't tell from here," Lauren said.

"It's much too large to be any indigenous animal," Noah said.

I knew right away what it was. I tried to convince myself that it was something else, but it was pointless. There was no denying the truth. "It's one of the stockings," I said. And it meant that someone's presents had missed the swap.

☘ CHAPTER EIGHTEEN ☘

I'M PRETTY SURE everyone had the same thought: Is that my stocking? That's the natural reaction to have when something goes wrong like that. It's like when you're out at a restaurant or the movies and one of the workers announces that a car in the parking lot left its lights on. Immediately, just about every adult thinks, if only for a split second, that it's their car. You can tell by the looks on their faces. Sometimes, I even think it might be my car. Then I remember that I'm just a kid, and I don't even have a car. That's basically what happened. I froze for a moment, thinking that it might be my stocking, before quickly realizing that I knew for a fact that it wasn't. I specifically remembered switching out my gifts.

"Grab it," I said to Ryan, who was the closest to the tree.

Ryan yanked the stocking free. All of the cousins held their breath as he searched for the name on the front. He found it and sighed. "Sorry, Josh."

Josh looked to his feet in disappointment.

"How'd this happen?" Claire asked.

"I don't know," I said.

"I do," Lauren said. She turned to me. "Remember when the sled got stuck? That had to be why we were stuck. And then when we pulled the sled free, the stocking must've fallen off."

"You're right. And we were in such a hurry, we never bothered to count the stockings."

"What are we going to do?" Noah said.

"I don't know," I said. "Let's just get everything back to the tree house and we can figure it out there."

Everyone agreed that we weren't likely to come up with any solutions on the spot. If anything, we were much more likely to get hypothermia, and so we silently and swiftly made our way back to my house.

🎁 🎁 🎁

When we returned to the tree house, Connor was already waiting for us. He bounced up and down with excitement as we heaved the stockings inside the tree house and then piled them in the corner of the room without a word.

After a few seconds, with none of us joining his celebration, Connor quickly came to a stop. Even though he was just six years old, he was perceptive enough to know that something was wrong. "What's up?" he said. "Why isn't everyone happy? You did it. We did it!"

"Not completely," I said. "We didn't get Josh's presents."

"What?" All of Connor's enthusiasm immediately vanished. "Why not? What are we gonna do?"

"We don't know yet. There might not be anything we can do."

"That's not true," Lauren said. "We can go back. We can get his stocking."

"Are you kidding me? You can't be serious," I said. "It's not like we can just waltz through the back door again and be like, 'Hey, Grandma and Grandpa, sorry to burst in, but we forgot to steal some of our presents back.'"

"I totally agree," Lauren said.

"Good."

"That's why we need a new plan."

"No, we don't." A lot of thoughts had passed through my mind on our march back as I struggled to devise a way to right our wrong. And while I hadn't come up with a workable solution just yet, the one thing that I was certain of was that we weren't going back. "What we need is—"

Before I could finish, Lauren snapped her fingers, cutting me off. "I got it!" she said, energized by her new plan. "It's past seven. Which means that Grandpa already went to the bathroom. Which also means the window is cracked, and we can go through there."

"The motion sensors give us a clear path," Ryan noted, warming up to the idea. "And there's that little bay window with a roof right below the bathroom. We could climb up there, no problem."

"Slow down," I said. I knew I needed to put the brakes on their rapidly forming plan as fast as possible. "Even if we could do that, Grandma and Grandpa will still be there, the Toys for Tots people will probably be there any minute, and our parents are gonna start wondering where we are, if they aren't already. It's way too risky."

"The presents are worth the risk," Lauren said.

"No, they aren't," I said. "No score is perfect. Ours was far from it. We were lucky that we pulled it off without getting busted, and we planned it for almost a month. There's no guarantee we'll be as lucky the next time. And if anything goes just a little bit wrong, we'll all lose our presents again."

Lauren was about to counter my point when Josh muttered, "It's okay, guys." He cleared his throat and then continued, "I don't need my presents."

His words stunned all of the cousins. It wasn't just what he'd said—the fact that he was willingly giving up his gifts—but that he'd said anything at all. It'd been so long since any of us had heard him speak that we hardly recognized his voice. It was actually a lot deeper than I'd remembered it being.

"None of us actually need our presents," Lauren said to Josh, "but you deserve yours just as much as any of us."

"I really think we should just listen to Josh," I said. "I mean, he hasn't said anything during the whole time we've been working on this job. If he says it's okay, it's gotta be okay."

Lauren shot me a nasty look. "Are you saying you're out?"

"No," I said. "All I'm saying is that we're on the corner, and there's heat on the other corner, or the other side. We need to walk away from heat, or we'll get burned. You know, by the heat on that side." I'd totally butchered Robert De Niro's line, but I was hoping it would be enough to persuade Lauren to reconsider her new plan.

It wasn't.

"What if your presents were on the line?" Lauren asked, her eyes narrowing. "Would you have a problem with the heat then?"

I knew the answer to that question right away: Of course not! But I also knew that I couldn't say that to Lauren. I tried to change the subject. "How's this?" I said. "What if each of us just gives him some of our presents to make up for his loss? That's not a bad idea, right?"

"Fine," Lauren said with knowing smirk. "Just give Josh your PlayStation, and we can all forget about going back."

"Uh," I stuttered. There was no way I could say yes, but at the same time I couldn't say no. I had no good moves to make. If we were playing chess, she would have already called checkmate.

Thankfully, Josh stepped in and saved me. "I couldn't take that," he said.

"I *would* give it to him," I said, trying to sound genuine, "but it sounds like he doesn't want it. I'm not gonna force him to take it."

My body must have betrayed me and told my true feelings because Lauren didn't buy what I'd said for one second. "No. You wouldn't," she said and shook her head. "That's all this was ever about: your presents. Your little PS4." She poked her finger into my chest. "You never cared about us or us getting our presents. The last thing you'd ever do is risk your presents for anyone else. All you care about is yourself."

I'd had enough of her badgering, and her finger was really starting to dig into my sternum. I totally lost my cool. "So what?" I said and slapped her hand away. "All of you are the reason I lost my presents in the first place. I didn't do anything. If you ask me, you deserve to not get your presents."

"Wow! The truth finally comes out." Lauren chuckled to herself. "I guess I wasn't wrong about you." She turned to the rest of the cousins. "I'm going back for Josh's presents. Anyone who wants to join me is welcome to come. Everyone else can stay with Mitch and play video games."

I figured she was gonna regret the last part. Even though I didn't sign off on her offer to let the others partake in my PlayStation, there was no way they would pass up the opportunity to test-drive my brand-new gaming system . . . or so I thought.

"I'm always there for the team, and my brother," Noah said as he threw his arm around Josh.

Josh smiled.

"Leave no man or his presents behind," Ryan said. "I'm in."

"Me too," Claire said. "I already have a ton of stuff anyway."

"All right," Lauren said, "let's do this." She gave me one last dirty look. "Have fun with your little video games." And then she and her crew climbed out of the tree house.

"Wait for me," Connor said as he went to follow after them.

I stopped my little brother. "Hey. Where are you going?"

"That's a clown question, bro," Connor said. "I'm going with them. And you should too."

Connor exited the tree house, leaving me all alone. I watched from the window as the cousins trekked off into the snow.

After they'd disappeared, I retrieved my PlayStation from the oversize stocking. I didn't feel the same joy that I'd felt when I'd first found it under my parents' bed, or even when I'd swapped it out. All I felt was guilt.

I slipped my gift back into the stocking, climbed out of the tree house, and headed inside my house.

My parents were nowhere to be found.

I found out later that they'd gone to the adults-only party across the street at the Griffins'. It was their first time attending the annual party. They'd been invited every year before but would always decline so that we could spend time as a family.

My mom had baked a couple trays of her famous sugar cookies before she'd left. As I stared at the golden-brown treats, it dawned on me that I'd been so dedicated to my holiday boycott, that I hadn't even had a single sugar cookie.

During a regular holiday season, I would have already had at least a couple dozen. And at that point on Christmas Eve, we'd be busy slathering them with icing to leave for Santa. I decided, since no one was there to catch me, that I could finally have one.

I grabbed the biggest cookie and took a bite. I'd forgotten how tasty they were. They were the perfect blend of chewy and crunchy. My mom truly had a skill. Unfortunately, even the deliciousness of the cookie couldn't pull me from my funk.

My spirits were lifted a little when I remembered my best friend Wes. I was certain that he would be pumped for me. I knew he'd be down to come over and play a couple rounds of *Call of Duty* right away. I grabbed the phone and dialed his number.

His mother picked up. "Hello?" she said.

"Oh, hi, Mrs. Jackson," I said. "Is Wes around?"

"Actually, he went caroling with his church group. But he should be back around 8:30 or so."

Disappointed, I slid my hand into my coat pocket. My fingers grazed what felt like a clump of ice. Instinctively, I retracted my hand a little, and then reached further and removed the freezing object from my pocket. It was the medal that Lauren had given me. I'd forgotten that I slipped it in my pocket when I'd gotten dressed. For good luck, I guess. So much for that working out.

"Do you want me to tell him you called?" Mrs. Jackson said.

I barely heard her. I was too focused on the medal.

"Mitch?" she said. "Hello?"

"Sorry," I said, snapping to.

"Do you want me to tell him you called?" she asked again.

"Uh, you don't have to. I'll just call his cell phone."

"Okay. Well, tell your parents Merry Christmas for me."

"I will. Merry Christmas to you too."

I hung up the phone. My attention shifted back to the Floor General medal and to what Lauren had said when she gave it to me. I replayed the hurtful things that I'd said about my cousins being the reason that I'd lost my presents, and that they didn't deserve to get theirs. I also replayed the food fight, hoping to convince myself that I'd been justified in what I'd said.

I remembered the look that Connor had given me, asking for approval before he fired the first shot in the infamous food battle, and how I'd just shrugged. I'd failed in my duties as a big brother. With this memory came the harsh realization that my hands weren't as clean as I'd thought. The whole thing had been just as much my fault as anyone else's.

❄ CHAPTER NINETEEN ❄

I DON'T KNOW if you've ever played the game Telephone. But if you have, you know how stories can quickly change the more times other people tell them. Since I wasn't there for the second heist attempt, it probably makes more sense for someone who was actually there to tell you what happened. With that in mind, I'll hand over the reins to Lauren.

Hey there, Lauren Wetterling here. I'm not sure what Mitch told you about me. But if he said anything bad, it's not true, and I'm gonna punch him later. Just kidding. I don't do that anymore, to Mitch or to anyone else. You probably shouldn't hit anyone either, but you probably already knew that.

So, after Mitch bailed on us, which is totally what he did, we made the long hike back to our grandparents' house. The only thing that kept all of us going was sheer determination . . . and the fact that I made sure to ride anyone who started to slack off.

When we got to our grandparents' house, we spotted them through the family room window. They were sitting on the couch, watching *It's a Wonderful Life* on TV.

Knowing Grandpa, he was probably still complaining about the chain lock for the back door being left unlocked while Grandma was just trying to enjoy the movie.

Noah had a pair of binoculars, which I used to get a better view of the TV. I'd seen the movie tons of times and recognized the part right away. "George is at the bridge," I said. "The movie should keep them preoccupied for at least another half hour."

"That's more than enough time," Ryan said.

I shifted my focus to the bathroom window on the second floor. The window was cracked open, just as I'd expected. "We're good on the entry too," I said as I handed Noah his binoculars. "Ryan and I are going inside. The rest of you guys need to keep an eye on Grandma and Grandpa. If they leave the family room, you let us know."

"How?" Claire asked. "If we call you on your cell, they could hear the ring or vibration."

"Good point," I said. "Can any of you do a bird call?"

Claire arched her eyebrow. "Seriously?"

"Yeah, seriously." I didn't think it was that crazy of an ask.

Josh shook his head.

"I can do a duck," Connor said. He quietly showed off his duck call, "Quack. Quack."

"All of the ducks migrated south several months ago," Noah pointed out. "Besides, ducks don't actually say 'quack.'"

"Quack," Connor repeated.

"What about an owl?" Ryan said. "Owls are easy. Anyone can do them."

"Yeah," I agreed. "Just go whooo whooo. Okay?"

"Whooo whooo," the little cousins all said at once.

I saw Grandpa turn his head on the couch.

"Not now," I said, holding a finger to my lips to quiet them. "Wait until you need to say it. But that's good."

They all grinned.

"All right, Ryan and I are going in," I said.

Since he hadn't expected us to need it, Ryan never bothered to mark off the second path with pinecones. So before we could actually make our way, we needed a little help from the Human Computer. That's my nickname for Noah. Although, with the way that he quickly calculated the path we needed to take to get to the back window from the little info that Ryan gave him, I could probably start calling him the Human Protractor too.

"You're sure this is right?" I said as we waited on the fringe of the safe zone.

Noah extended his arms and double-checked his calculations. "If Ryan was correct about the 68 degree angle of the path, then I am positive this is the precise route."

"Okay," I said. Deep down—well, not really that deep down—I was still a little nervous that either Noah or Ryan had been off in their calculations. I carefully lifted my foot and, even more carefully than I'd lifted it, took my first step into the backyard.

To my relief, the motion lights didn't go off. I sighed and then took my second step. Still good. "Good job, Noah," I said.

He smiled and nodded.

"What about me?" Ryan said.

"Good job to you too," I said.

I continued to tiptoe to the back of the house. Ryan followed my footprints as he carried the stocking filled with Josh's decoy presents.

We made it to the back of the house without tripping any of the sensors. Ryan had been right about the window ledge. There were a couple ledges that made it an easy climb to the cracked bathroom window just above us.

"I can go first," Ryan said. "Once I get inside, I'll throw down the string of lights. Then you tie it to the stocking, and I'll pull it up."

"Good thinking," I said. "And good call on bringing the lights."

Before we left Mitch's tree house, Ryan had wrapped a couple strings of lights over his shoulder like a rope. When I asked him why he was bringing them, he said he wanted to be prepared. It was the only thing he'd remembered from his four years as a Cub Scout, and it was a good thing he did.

Ryan made quick work of the ledges. In no time, he was at the window. He carefully lifted the window and slipped inside. No sooner had he dropped in than his head popped back out. He coughed violently.

"Are you okay?" I said.

"No," Ryan said, still hacking. "It smells worse than a Chinese restaurant's dumpster in here." He cupped his hands and attempted to waft the foul air out of the bathroom.

"Stop it!" I whispered. "And be quiet! Just breathe through your mouth."

"I don't want to taste it!"

"You won't taste it."

"I'm pretty sure I will. But either way, I don't want to find out."

"We don't have time to debate this. Just breathe through your shirt and toss me the lights."

Ryan lifted his shirt to cover his nose and mouth. He unraveled the string of lights and lowered them down from the window. I grabbed the end of the string and tied it around the stocking. I gave Ryan a thumbs-up, and he pulled the stocking up to the window.

I wasn't as skilled at climbing up the ledges as Ryan, but I didn't do that bad either. Once I got to the top, I slipped inside the window.

"You're lucky," Ryan said, his eyes watering. "Most of the smell is gone already."

"Good to know," I said, breathing through my shirt and mouth just to be safe. I carefully lowered the window to its original position. "Let's do this. As fast and as quiet as possible."

"Let's rock and roll," Ryan said. "Quietly, of course."

We tiptoed out of the bathroom and across the hall to our grandparents' bedroom. Ryan gently tugged the cord for the retractable stairs.

The stairs exploded from the ceiling, falling way faster than they had before. Thanks to my well-trained reflexes, I was able to step in and catch them. They let out a high-pitched creaking as they came to a sudden stop. The fact that we were trying so hard to be quiet only made the noise seem more amplified than it really was.

Ryan and I froze, waiting to see if the owl calls would follow.

They didn't.

After a couple seconds, we climbed up the stairs and into the attic. While we swapped out the presents, I couldn't help but think about how Mitch had bailed on us. "Can you believe Mitch?" I said. "What a jerk."

"Yeah," Ryan agreed. "It was a jerk move. But at the same time—"

"You're not actually gonna defend him, are you?"

"No. I'm just saying—"

I involuntarily shot Ryan a harsh glare—force of habit, I guess. He totally shifted gears.

"You know what?" Ryan said. "I don't know what I'm saying. Let's just finish up and get out of here. Okay?"

"Yeah," I agreed. As annoyed as I still was, he was right. It wasn't the time to vent. We needed to swap out the remaining presents and get to safety. I'd have plenty of time to rant about how much of a jerk Mitch was later, probably my whole life.

We silently switched out the rest of Josh's presents.

"That's all of them," Ryan said as he stuffed the final present into the stocking.

"Let's get out of here," I said.

Ryan nodded and then slung the stocking over his shoulder and started down the attic stairs.

I vividly remember watching him as I followed just behind, thinking to myself that he shouldn't be skipping steps like he was.

Sure enough, his heel slipped on the very last step, and his boot slammed onto the floor with a booming thud. My stomach dropped. Ryan and I went catatonic.

While the sound of the retractable staircase falling had only seemed loud because we were being so careful, there was no way that Ryan's foot pounding the wood planks hadn't echoed throughout the downstairs.

We waited for the owl alarm. But to both of our surprises, it didn't sound. We waited for a few more seconds, but there still wasn't even the slightest peep.

"Maybe we're okay," Ryan whispered.

"Maybe," I said, and then carefully completed my descent down the attic stairs, one step at a time. "That was really close."

"Yeah," Ryan agreed, and then shut the staircase as delicately as possible.

We both tiptoed toward the hall, and that's when the hoots came flying in, in rapid succession.

"Whooo! Whooo! Whooo! Whooo!" the cousins bellowed from the backyard, all of them in different pitches and out of sync. It sounded like four rabid owls were fighting over a dead mouse or something. As terrible as the noise was on the ears, its meaning was even more unpleasant: Grandpa was on his way.

✦ CHAPTER TWENTY ✦

IT'S STILL LAUREN here, just in case you forgot. Forgive me if Mitch has already talked about "fight, flight, or freeze." Being in the same grade and a most of the same classes, we learn the same stuff. Anyway, it's my opinion that sometimes you gotta do your own thing, and the best option is just to hide your keister—as Grandpa likes to call it— as fast as humanly possible. Maybe that counts as flight, but who knows. I'm not an expert. I've barely spent a class period learning about it, and I wasn't really paying that much attention.

"You take the guest room," I told Ryan as the "whooo"s kept coming, louder and louder. "I'll hide in the bathroom."

Ryan nodded, and then we split up.

I climbed into the bathtub and closed the curtain. There was a tiny tear in the vinyl that gave me a clear view of the top of the stairs and of Ryan, who was frantically searching for a hiding spot in the guest room.

I heard Grandpa shout to Grandma from the bottom of the stairs. "You might not have heard something, but I sure did. And I don't know where those damn owls came from either, but they're lucky I can't find my BB gun. A couple pellets would quiet them real quick!"

The sound of Grandpa's feet hitting each of the old wooden steps echoed up the stairway. My nerves spiraled more and more out of control with each resulting creak. I could actually hear my heart beating in my head and feel it in my hands.

How crazy is that? It's not like I haven't dealt with pressure before either. I've hit plenty of game-winning shots without even the slightest change in my pulse, but this was something else. This was new to me, and I didn't like it one bit.

As shaken as I was, I could only imagine how Ryan must've felt. At least I was covered by the curtain; he was still out in the open. Ryan had yet to find a hiding spot when I saw the top of Grandpa's bald head pop up into view. Ryan must've known he was close too because he froze, standing as still as a marble statue.

I watched anxiously as Grandpa continued to the top of the stairs. He took a second to catch his breath and then peered into his bedroom. "Everything seems fine," he said to himself.

That was exactly what I wanted to hear. Now all he needed to do was turn around and head back down the stairs.

But instead, Grandpa just lingered in the hall, continuing to mumble to himself. "But I know that I heard something."

He started toward the guest room where Ryan was, still without a hiding spot.

I closed my eyes, convinced it was only a matter of seconds before Ryan would be busted and the whole job would be over. I prepared myself for Ryan's screams, or Grandpa's screams when he discovered his grandson had become a home intruder, but the only thing I heard was the front doorbell.

I slowly opened my eyes. Grandpa was literally inches from discovering Ryan, whose face was redder than Santa's sleigh. Ryan had clearly been holding his breath ever since Grandpa had made it to the hall, and judging by the color of his cheeks, he was super close to passing out.

"Do you want me to get that?" Grandma shouted from downstairs.

Grandpa stood there for a second. "That's okay," he said. "I got it." He started back down the stairs.

Ryan let out his breath and doubled over.

"Do you know who it is?" Grandma shouted.

"I have no idea," Grandpa shouted back.

Neither did I, but I sure was glad they were there. Whoever was waiting outside, they had totally saved us. As Grandpa opened the front door, we all got our answer.

A group of carolers immediately burst into song. *"We wish you a merry Christmas! We wish you a merry Christmas! We wish you a merry Christmas and a happy New Year!"*

I crawled out of the tub and then hurried into the hallway as the carolers continued to sing. I peeked down the stairs toward the foyer to check on our grandparents. They were both totally distracted by the carolers.

I waved to Ryan and mouthed, "Let's go!"

He scurried across the hall and into the bathroom.

I don't know why I did what I did next—maybe it was because I hadn't heard any Christmas carols in a while and it sounded nice, or maybe I just wanted to get a better view of who I should be thanking for saving us—but before I turned back to head into the bathroom, I took one last look at the group of carolers. When I did, I couldn't believe what I saw. I shook my head and blinked twice to make sure it wasn't a hallucination.

In the group was Mitch's friend Will, or Wes, or whatever his name is. However, he wasn't the only face I recognized. Next to him, singing along with a huge smile on his goofy little face, was Mitch.

Who were you expecting, Justin Bieber and Selena Gomez? Of course it was me. Oh, yeah, I'm back, by the way. Hope you guys enjoyed Lauren filling in some of the holes for you. Pretty crazy how close they were to getting busted, right?

Anyway, I guess you could say that my guilt had gotten the best of me, and I knew that I couldn't just leave my cousins hanging. I'm sure some really smart person has a great quote on guilt, but since I don't know it I'll just say that guilt sucks, and the only way to get rid of it is to do something to make up for whatever you did and are feeling guilty about.

That's exactly what I'd decided to do. After talking to Wes's mom, I called Wes's cell to see where they were. When I found out they were only a couple blocks from my grandparents' house, I told him to stall the group and wait for me. I obviously hadn't known the mess that Lauren and Ryan had gotten themselves into, but I figured that a little distraction couldn't hurt. I've never been more right in my whole life.

After we sang a couple songs for my grandparents, I hung around with the carolers for a few more houses, just to make sure that I didn't look too suspicious, and then said goodbye to Wes and the others and hurried home.

All of the cousins were waiting for me at the tree house. They gave me a real hero's welcome. Lauren tore me away from the group and pulled me in for a bear hug.

"You were right," I said. "It was worth the risk. We're a team."

"No," Lauren said. "We're more than a team. We're family."

"Yeah, we are," Connor said, joining our hug.

"And as a family," Ryan said, "we got all of our presents back!"

"We sure did," I said.

All of the cousins simultaneously turned to the corner of the tree house with toothy grins. Some of the presents were stacked and some were still in their stockings, but they were all there. It felt great, for a second, and then the feeling started to fade along with our smiles.

"This doesn't feel right," I said. "Something's missing."

The others considered my observation for a couple seconds. "He's right," Lauren agreed.

Another couple seconds passed.

Connor's eyes lit up. "Duh!" he said. "We don't have a tree."

We all shook our heads and chuckled. It was so obvious.

"Of course," I said. "We need a tree."

"Yeah," Ryan said. "Everyone knows you can't have Christmas without a tree, right?"

"There's a little forest not too far from here," I said. "There are tons of pine trees. I'm sure no one would even notice if we cut one down."

"Then what are we waiting for?" Lauren said. "Let's get to it."

🎁 🎁 🎁

I knew the nearby woods pretty well. Wes and I had hang out there a lot when we were younger and used make our own bows and arrows.

"You weren't lying," Ryan said as we arrived at the patch of pines that I'd mentioned.

The tree selection was actually better than I'd remembered. It might have just been that all of the snow made them look even better than usual. Whatever the reasion, it sure made for a beautiful winter wonderland.

"This one looks nice," Lauren said as she examined what was probably the best of the lot.

"That's a Fraser fir," Noah said. "They don't get much better than that."

"It's pretty full. Great shape," Claire said as she scanned the tree with her critical eye. "I'd say it's better than the one my parents picked out. Not that they're known for their taste."

Ryan gave the tree a shake. "It's got a good, sturdy base too."

"The pleasure is all yours," I said as I offered Ryan the handsaw that I'd retrieved from my garage before we started our trek.

"Don't mind if I do." Ryan took the saw and then got to work cutting the tree.

We used my sled to transport the tree back to the tree house and then worked together to hoist it through the tiny hatch door.

Ryan and I balanced the tree in the corner of the tree house while the rest of the cousins guided us from the other side.

"That look good?" I asked.

"Maybe a little more to the left," Noah said.

Ryan and I angled the tree an inch to the left.

"How's that?" I asked.

"Better?" Ryan added.

"Yeah," Lauren said, grinning. "It's perfect."

It really was. It was a great tree. It fit perfectly snug in the corner, with just a little room between the top of the tree and the ceiling. It also had a fresh piney scent that filled the tree house and brought the smiles back to all of our faces.

However, just like before, the joy was temporary, and it was only a matter of seconds before our smiles had all but faded.

"There's still something missing," Noah said.

"I was just gonna say the same thing," I said. Honestly, I was. I'm not saying that to try to sound smart. I didn't know what was missing, but it was definitely something.

Claire snapped her fingers. "OMG! It's so obvi. We still gotta decorate the tree."

"Yeah," Lauren agreed. "We can't just have a plain tree. That's not Christmas at all."

"What is with us?" Noah said as he shook his head. "I cannot believe we forgot that."

"Seriously," I said. "I guess we're so far removed

from the Christmas spirit that we're forgetting even the most obvious stuff."

On one hand, our oversight was unbelievable. But on the other hand, it made perfect sense. After all, that's what happens when you stop doing anything: You get rusty. And we had built up some serious Christmas rust.

"I think my parents are still gone," I said. "We can grab some of our ornaments from inside and use the lights that we already have."

"Let's do it," Lauren said.

We all sprinted inside the house and then strategically plucked ornaments from the boxes that were stacked next to the tree. We made sure to leave my parents' favorites and to take the same amount from each box so that they'd be less likely to notice that any were missing.

We worked together to string the lights and decorate our tree with the borrowed ornaments. Once everything was in order, it was time to give it some juice.

"You guys ready for this?" I said with a grin.

They all nodded excitedly.

I plugged the lights into the extension cord that we'd been using for the space heater. The tree lit up in sparkling holiday splendor.

"Wow," Claire said. "It looks fab."

"Totes," Noah said. "Totes."

The rest of us just nodded our heads in agreement. We admired the tree in silence for a good ten seconds, but wouldn't you know, even that enjoyment came to an end.

Ryan shook his head. "We're—"

"Stop," Lauren said, cutting him off. "I already know what we're missing: Christmas music."

"Yes!" I said. "We need some good old holiday tunes."

"Once we have that, we'll have everything, right?" Ryan said.

"I can't think of anything else," Claire said.

"Me either," Connor agreed.

"I have Pandora on my phone," Lauren said. She retrieved her phone and opened the app. "What do you know? I even have a Christmas station saved from last year." She hit play.

Darlene Love's "Christmas (Baby, Please Come Home)" started to blast from the phone's speakers.

"I love this song," I said. It had been in my top five Christmas songs for the past couple years. While I'd mostly listened to the U2 version, the original was pretty much just as good.

"Me too," Lauren agreed. "It's one of my favorites."

We all beamed, nodding along to the melody and the magic of Darlene Love's voice.

"Hey, it's snowing outside," Ryan said, pointing out the obvious similarity between the song's lyrics and our situation.

"We have a lot of people here too," Noah added.

The song continued. Connor got a suspicious look on his mug. "Wait a second," he grumbled. "Who's this baby, and why won't they come home?"

"I don't know," Lauren said.

We all listened to the lyrics even closer. As the song kept playing, it was clear that it wasn't the happy holiday tune that we'd thought it was. It was a sad song about someone spending Christmas without the one they loved.

By the time everyone realized what the song was really about, the smiles had completely vanished from all of our faces once more, leaving a collection of blank stares and frowns.

"Well, this is just depressing," Claire groaned.

"She's right," I said. "We should probably shut it off."

Lauren stopped the song. "I guess I never really listened to the words."

"Me either," I said. "I still like the music, though."

"Yeah."

We stood in silence for almost a minute. I don't know about the others, but the lyrics kept replaying in my head. And it just made me more and more bummed out. It wasn't how I wanted to feel at all, not then or ever. There was only one thing that I could think of that I was certain would fix my mood.

"You know what? Forget all that stuff," I said, doing my best to bring some energy back into the group. "We don't really need music or anything else. We got our presents, don't we? That's all we need!"

The others cheered in excitement.

"Let's just open them, okay?" I said.

Everyone nodded as they continued to cheer.

"All right," I said. "Who wants to go first?"

Instead of the usual fight to be the first one to open a gift, it was like in the movies when the record skips. The excitement instantly disappeared and everyone went back to being silent. You seriously could have heard a pin drop, maybe even something quieter than a pin, like, I don't know, a smaller pin?

After a couple seconds of no one stepping up, I said, "Come on. Who's first? Lauren, my co-lead? What do you say?"

"Well, we usually let whoever finds the Christmas pickle go first," Lauren said.

"Same here," Noah said.

"Well, we don't have a Christmas pickle," I said. "So we can't really do that. Plus, we couldn't exactly hide it either."

"It's okay. I can wait until after everyone else goes," Lauren said.

"Me too," Noah said.

"Fine," I said. "What about you, Claire? Do you want to do the honors?"

"I'm an only child," Claire said. "I go first all the time. But this was your idea, so maybe you should go first."

"I appreciate that," I said. "But I really just have the one present. And I already know what it is, anyway. So there's no surprise."

"I'd rather wait too," Claire said.

"Suit yourself," I said, and then turned to Connor and Josh. "What about you guys? Do either of you want to go first?"

Josh just shook his head.

"What he said, or didn't say," Connor said. "Someone else can go first."

"Ryan?" I said. "You're the last one. Oldest first."

"No thanks," Ryan said. "I'm in no hurry."

I couldn't help but be frustrated. Did I need to point out the obvious, that someone needed to step up and go first? I guess I did. "Obviously, we can all wait," I said. "It's been established. But you guys realize that one of us is gonna have to go first, right? It's just the way it is."

No one said a word.

After a few seconds, Noah finally spoke up. "Not necessarily," he said, and then turned back toward the pile of presents.

The rest of us matched his sullen gaze. There was no getting around the fact that something was still missing. It was the feeling of Christmas that came from all the little things that we were used to doing leading up to Christmas, the things that helped build up our Christmas spirit.

"I just realized I haven't even watched *Christmas Vacation* or *Home Alone* once this year," Ryan said.

"Don't forget about *A Christmas Story*," Lauren said.

"Good call. That's a classic."

"I missed the Christmas parade," Claire said. "I totally heart the Christmas parade."

"Samesies," Noah agreed.

"I didn't go to see Santa," Connor said. "I told my dad I didn't want to go, and the elf on the shelf saw it all."

"My parents don't like when I eat chocolate," Josh said. "But it was good chocolate."

As I thought about Josh's words, I realized that it wasn't just our spirit that was missing. While we'd become closer as cousins than we'd ever been, we were still missing the most important piece of our holiday puzzle: our parents.

"I wish my parents were here," I said. The room went silent. I continued, "This will never feel right."

Admitting the truth opened the floodgates for the rest of the cousins. Lauren kicked things off. "This isn't Christmas," she said. "It's just a bunch of toys."

"I don't really even want my presents," Claire said. "And I definitely don't deserve them. I was a jerk."

"So was I," Connor said. "I don't deserve them either."

The rest of the cousins all chimed in with similar sentiments. I was the last one to agree. As hard as it was for me to admit it, I didn't deserve the PlayStation, especially not after all of the messed up things that I'd been willing to do just to get it.

"Well, what should we do?" Ryan asked.

"I'll do whatever the team wants to do," Noah said.

Everyone turned their eyes toward me, looking for a suggestion. "I think I have an idea," I said and shook my head. I couldn't believe that I was actually thinking of doing what I was thinking of doing.

❄ CHAPTER TWENTY-ONE ❄

CHARITY IS A funny thing. When you donate to charity or volunteer your time because someone else makes you to do it, not only does that not really count as charity, it also makes the charity feel like a chore or work. In the past, whenever I was forced to volunteer for school or church, I always complained and never got anything out of it. The same thing went for when my parents decided they were donating my Christmas presents to charity. However, when you give because you really want to and because you know it's the right thing to do, the feeling you get in return can actually be pretty amazing.

Lauren called the Toys for Tots number listed on the flyer that was still hanging the tree house. The operator said that we were lucky because they had just enough time and space for one more pickup. Lauren told them to meet us at the park a couple blocks from my house. No sense in getting busted with our presents while we were giving them away, right?

The donation truck arrived at the drop a couple minutes after we did.

"I got a little nervous when you told me to meet you at this park," the driver said. "These toys aren't hot, are they?"

For those of you who've only heard someone use "hot" to describe the temperature or someone's looks, it also means "stolen" in heist-speak.

All of the cousins shared looks of concern. None of us had considered the legal ramifications of stealing your own presents, or if it still qualifies as breaking and entering if it's your own grandparents' house. For all we knew, this driver was an undercover police officer, going around busting bad donations.

I swallowed hard. "No, uh, why do you ask?"

The driver laughed and slapped me on the back. "I'm just joking, kid. You should've seen your face."

"Oh, yeah," I said, loosening up. "I knew that. Ha ha. Great joke."

We all faked chuckles, playing along.

"All right," the driver said. "If you guys don't mind loading up the goods, I gotta get back to the wife and kids."

"Sure," I said, and then turned to my cousins. "I don't mind going first this time."

"Let's give him a second alone," Lauren said to the others.

"Thanks," I said, and then made my way to the back of the donation truck. It was jam-packed with presents. If someone was looking for a real score—I'm talking about the silver tuna—that would be the place to hit, but that's beside the point.

I ran my hand across the wrapped PlayStation, just like I had the first time I'd discovered it under my parents' bed. This might sound a little weird, but I felt the need to say goodbye. "We could have had some great times," I said. "But it just wouldn't have been right. Maybe in another life, or maybe just another Christmas."

I gently laid the gift in the bed of the truck. My cousins patted me on the back as I returned to the curb. One by one, they added most of their presents to the stash while setting aside the gifts that we'd promised Floyd.

"That's it," Ryan said as he deposited his last present in the truck.

"Just one more matter of business," the driver said. He handed me a slip of paper.

"What's this?" I said, my heart skipping a beat. In the back of my mind, I still hadn't let go of the idea that he might be an undercover cop, and was expecting it to be a citation or some kind of warrant to search my bedroom. Soon he'd flash his badge, cuff us, and then tell us about how they were on to us from the start.

"It's a receipt," the driver said. "Donations are tax-deductible."

"Oh, cool," I said, relieved. "But I'm pretty sure I don't pay taxes."

"Lucky you. Just give it to your parents. I'm assuming this was their donation anyway, right?"

"Oh, yeah. Of course it was."

The driver closed the cargo door. "All right. Well, you kids have a merry Christmas, and happy holidays."

"Happy holidays," we all said back.

He gave a wave and then hopped in his truck.

We all watched as the truck pulled away and our presents disappeared in the night.

"I never would have thought that I'd actually feel better giving my presents away than I would opening them," Lauren said, "but I really do."

"My parents do always say that it's better to give than to receive," Noah said.

"Yeah, well, parents like to say a lot of dumb stuff," Ryan said. "But in this case, I guess they're right."

"Yeah," I agreed.

"We should probably all get home to our parents while there's still a little bit of Christmas Eve left," Claire said.

"Good thinking."

"Ryan and I can drop off Floyd's sled and give him his cut on the way back to our house," Lauren said.

"Are you sure about that?" I said.

"Yeah," Lauren said.

"Just remember, the best way to survive a shark attack is to punch it in the nose."

Lauren chuckled at my joke. "I have another plan," she said. "If he acts like a jerk, I'll just take the high road. Tell him Merry Christmas and walk away."

"That's a better idea. It'll definitely mess with his head. Let me know how it goes."

"Of course."

We all said our goodbyes and then headed our separate ways.

When Connor and I returned home, our parents were still at the party. As I looked around the empty house, I realized that Connor and I weren't the only ones who'd been slacking on our Christmas, it was clear that our parents had been too. There was still tons of work that needed to get done for the house to be completely ready for the big day.

Finally filled with Christmas spirit, we decided to do something about the subpar decorations. I threw on some cheerful Christmas music, and then Connor and I got to work setting up the rest of the decorations. Once we were done decorating, I whipped up some icing for the bare sugar cookies, using a recipe I found on the Internet. Usually, Connor and I would fight over who got to lick the mixer beaters, but I decided to be nice and let the little guy have them.

By chance, our parents returned just as Connor and I were wrapping up. They couldn't have been more surprised to find us setting a plate of cookies on the fireplace.

"What are you guys doing?" my dad said after his shock had finished settling in.

"We're just setting cookies out for Santa," I said. "Unless you were gonna use them for something else."

"No. Um, of course not," my mom stammered. "That's what they're for. I just didn't know if you guys still wanted to do that."

"Well, Connor figured it was a good idea," I said.

"Just because Santa isn't bringing us any presents doesn't mean he won't need to stop by for a little break," Connor explained and then nodded to the elf on the mantel. "You hear that, elf? I'm looking out for the big guy."

My parents smiled.

So did I. It had been a while since I remembered being that happy around them—Thanksgiving afternoon, to be exact.

"Plus," I said, "it never hurts to grease the wheels for next year, right?"

"Right," my dad agreed. He threw his arm around me and gave me a kiss on the forehead.

"Well, should we decorate the tree now?" I said.

"I'd love to," my mom said.

🎁 🎁 🎁

We laughed and sang along to every holiday album we owned as we filled the tree with ornaments. My dad even snuck in a couple of his favorite Christmas tunes, including one by The Ramones, a punk band that my mom really doesn't like, but she even sang along to that one.

When the last ornament was set on the tree, it was time for our final Christmas Eve tradition. Every year, just before we went to bed, my dad would start a fire and then we would all squeeze onto the couch and spend a half hour just admiring the tree.

"I think we did a great job decorating," my dad said.

"Me too," Connor said.

"Same here," I agreed.

My mom was always a little more particular. She studied the tree for a moment.

"Is there something wrong, dear?" my dad asked.

My mom considered the tree for couple more seconds. "No," she said. "It's just . . . it looks like it's missing some ornaments. But we used everything that we have."

Connor and I shared a look. Whoops. We'd totally forgotten to remove the ornaments from the tree house tree. I made a mental note to remember to take care of them later.

My mom continued, "But it looks great. And this is great." She pulled Connor and me in tight.

"It definitely is," I agreed.

🎁 🎁 🎁

I don't think the Guinness Book of World Records keeps track of these kinds of things—they're more focused on stuff like the biggest flash mob or who has the longest toenails—but I swear I had to have set the record for fastest time to fall asleep for any kid under the age of eighteen on Christmas Eve. Some might argue that my record deserves an asterisk, since I knew that I wasn't getting any presents, but it's not like I wasn't excited for Christmas. I couldn't have been more excited to spend the day with my family; it just wasn't the same kind of nervous anticipation that keeps you tossing and turning all hours of the night. So as soon as my bedroom lights went out, so did I.

A healthy eight hours later, I woke up with a smile, feeling great. I cleaned up, combing my hair and brushing my teeth, and then threw on my Christmas best: a white button-down, my nicest V-neck sweater, and khaki pants.

When I got downstairs, the rest of my family was already up. They were sitting on the couch, still in their pajamas, watching A Christmas Story on TV. It just so happened to be on the great scene where Ralphie finally gets his BB gun.

"Look who decided to wake up," my mom said as I strolled into the family room.

Apparently, Connor had woken up at his usual Christmas time, proof that old habits are hard to break, especially for six-year-olds.

My mom continued, "I was wondering what was taking you so long."

"It takes a lot of work to look this good," I said.

"Hey, that's my line," my dad said.

I smiled. "So, what time is breakfast?"

"We aren't eating here," my mom said. "We're going to Grandma and Grandpa's."

"Oh, nice."

"We're gonna get ready as soon as the movie is over. Your father is even gonna be extra quick today. Right, Pat?"

"Of course," my dad said. "Although, everything is relative."

My mom just shook her head, and I joined my family on the couch to watch the rest of the movie.

Once the movie had ended, everyone else went upstairs to get ready, and I slipped downstairs to the basement to give Wes a call. "I don't know what to say," he said after I told him the news.

"You can just say Merry Christmas," I said.

"All right then, Merry Christmas."

"Merry Christmas to you too. How are the headphones?"

"Even better than I'd imagined. And I also got an iTunes gift card, which I wasn't expecting."

"It sounds like you were pleasantly surprised," I said.

"I was," Wes said with a chuckle.

"Me too," I said, smiling to myself. "I guess it is possible after all."

After making plans to hang out later, I headed back upstairs, where I watched *Home Alone* until it was time to leave.

🎁 🎁 🎁

Just like Thanksgiving, we were the last to arrive at my grandparents'. However, we weren't as late as before, and it didn't really seem to bother my mom like usual. When we got there, all of my extended family was packed in the entrance and dining room.

Lauren was the first person to greet me. "Merry Christmas," she said as she gave me a big hug.

"Merry Christmas," I said. "I'm actually kinda surprised we're doing the big family Christmas."

"Yeah, I figured after the Thanksgiving debacle we were gonna take the holidays off for a while. Or at least this one."

"Me too. But I'm really glad we didn't. It's great to have the whole family together."

"It really is. I can't believe—"

Before Lauren could finish, she was cut off by Aunt Jackie, who let loose one of her loud throat-clearings. "Excuse me," Aunt Jackie said. "If I could have your attention."

The room quieted.

Aunt Jackie continued, "Thank you. Now that we're all here, if everyone could please follow me."

Aunt Jackie and the rest of the adults headed for the family room. Lauren and I didn't move. We were both still trying to figure out what to make of the situation.

Noah and the rest of the cousins approached us. "Do either of you guys have any clue what this is about?" he whispered.

"I honestly have no idea," Lauren said.

"Me either," I said. "But I guess we're about to find out."

We followed our parents into the family room. They'd already formed a line, blocking off most of the room. All of us cousins huddled by the entrance.

"I know that everyone remembers what happened the last time we got together," Aunt Jackie said. "There was a huge mess, and we decided that all of you needed to learn a lesson."

"We know this was a really tough month for all of you," Aunt Denise chimed in. "But it was also really tough for us too."

Parents say that kind of stuff all the time. They claim that punishing you is actually harder on them than it is on you. I've never really bought that before, but I could tell by the look in Aunt Denise's eyes that she meant what she said. She even choked up a little.

"But," my mom said, stepping in, "you've all been so good, spending lots of time together and just getting along so well, that we decided that you more than learned your lesson and deserve to get your presents back."

Our parents parted down the middle, giving us a clear view of the corner of the room and our grandparents' Christmas tree. Under the tree were all of our presents. Or so our parents thought. Of course, we knew better, which is why we all just stood there, like a line of nutcracker statues on a fireplace.

"Merry Christmas, you guys," my mom said. "Who wants to go first?"

For a multitude of reasons, none of the cousins volunteered.

"Come on," Aunt Janet said. "One of you must want to go first."

I could feel all of the cousins' eyes shifting toward me. I turned to face them. I shook my head and chuckled. "I guess I will," I said, and then, for the first time in a long time, I did something that wasn't crazy. I didn't try to come up with a lie or a ridiculous way out of my predicament. I came clean and told my parents, aunts, uncles, and grandparents the truth, the whole truth, and nothing but the truth.

☃ EPILOGUE ☃

I'M NOT GOING to tell you what happened after I spilled the beans because the fact of the matter is it isn't important. It doesn't make any difference if my parents grounded me for the next two years, or if they applauded the fact that we'd donated all of our gifts. And don't try to read into the fact that I mentioned the grounding first.

Whether we were punished again or not isn't the point of the story. Really, there's more than one point. I mean, there's, like, a ton of points. Hopefully, you picked up on most of them.

One of the biggest things you should have taken away from my experience is something you hear old people say all of the time: Two wrongs don't make a right. As much as I hate to agree with adults, they know what they're talking about with that. The only thing that turns a wrong into a right is a right. Sometimes, it might even take two or three rights, or more than that.

Hopefully, if you were reading this, taking notes, and highlighting stuff, with the goal of pulling off a heist of your own, you've already decided to call it off. If you haven't, all I ask is that you at least consider trying to do a right first.

Instead of scheming like I did, think about the actions that caused you to end up where ever you are and what you can do, within the confines of the law, to correct them. Maybe tell your parents you're sorry for whatever you did and mean it. Maybe just tell them you love them, because hopefully you really do. That goes for everyone, not just the kids who might be in trouble. And don't stop with your parents either. Say I love you to your siblings, your grandparents, and all of your close friends. I promise you'll feel great when you do it.

After all, the biggest lesson I learned on my whole crazy ride was that the joy you get from a great present disappears a lot faster than you'd think. What's cool now isn't always cool later (see my tree house as an example). But the joy you get from a great relationship with your family lasts forever and is so much more rewarding. I guess it took me losing a PlayStation twice to fully realize that. But it's a lesson that's worth losing a million PlayStations to learn. Hopefully, you don't have to go through that. Hopefully, my story, and everything I've learned, can save you the trouble.

Acknowledgments

I'd like to thank everyone who took the time to read *Stealing Christmas*. I really appreciate your support. Hopefully you were able to get as much joy from reading the book as I received writing it. If you have a second, please rate the book on Amazon, and if you have two seconds, write a short and honest review. If you have three seconds, maybe add a review to Goodreads too.

My deepest thanks to ...

My parents, siblings, and in-laws for their love and support. My wife for being my sounding board and biggest cheerleader. Brian Levy for helping shape my career. Zoe Sandler for believing in me as a writer. Kristie Minke for her amazing illustrations. Lauren Leibowitz for cleaning up my grammar.

My beta readers for helping make the book the best it could be. And everyone—friends, family, and teachers—who has helped me get to where I am as a person and a writer.

Thanks!

About the Author

After graduating from the Johns Hopkins University, Matthew began working as an investment banker and was certain he had his whole life and career mapped out. He even had a twenty-year plan to prove it. But after a yearlong battle with cancer (he's been cured for over thirteen years now), Matthew realized that he needed to scrap his plans and focus on living in the moment. A few weeks later, he quit his job and began writing.

Since taking the leap, Matthew has written for film (*30 Minutes or Less*), television, and print, and loves crafting stories for all mediums and audiences. Matthew currently resides in Arlington, Virginia with his amazing wife. When he isn't writing, he enjoys spending time with his family and friends, and watching sports.

For more information on Matthew's upcoming projects, please visit matthewsullivanwriter.com and follow him on Twitter, Instagram, or Facebook:

Twitter: @sullivan_writer
Instagram: @sullivan_writer
facebook.com/matthewsullivanwriter